Stanislavski's Legacy

"Art is a human activity having for its purpose
the transmission to others of the highest and
best feelings to which men have risen."

LEO TOLSTOY

Also by Constantin Stanislavski

AN ACTOR PREPARES

AN ACTOR'S HANDBOOK

CREATING A ROLE

BUILDING A CHARACTER

MY LIFE IN ART

The Seagull PRODUCED BY STANISLAVSKI

STANISLAVSKI PRODUCES *Othello*

STANISLAVSKI ON OPERA

STANISLAVSKI'S LEGACY

STANISLAVSKI IN REHEARSAL

Stanislavski's Legacy

A Collection of Comments on a Variety of Aspects of an Actor's Art and Life *by*

CONSTANTIN STANISLAVSKI

REVISED AND EXPANDED EDITION

EDITED AND TRANSLATED BY

ELIZABETH REYNOLDS HAPGOOD

THEATRE ARTS BOOKS • *New York*

"Why Play Melodrama" was first published in *Theatre Arts* magazine, COPYRIGHT 1950 by Theatre Arts, and is republished with its permission.

"The Art of the Actor and the Art of the Director" was written for the *Encyclopaedia Britannica,* where it appeared, in another translation and slightly different form, between 1929 and 1956. The text as it is published in this book is translated directly from the Russian version found in Stanislavski's papers.

Library of Congress Catalog Card Number 68-16450

Published by
THEATRE ARTS BOOKS
333 Sixth Avenue, New York N.Y. 10014

Foreword to the Second Edition

As time goes on more and more pieces written by Stanislavski, including letters, notes, comments of various kinds, come to light and being published add to the rich bequest already enjoyed by all who are interested in or capable of profiting by his life's work. Thus this is not merely an afterglow which lingers briefly in a sunset sky.

Indeed, since *Stanislavski's Legacy* was first published in 1958, ostensibly to commemorate the twentieth anniversary of his death, the third volume of Stanislavski's main work came to light in three drafts, which were edited and put together with the help of Hermine Isaacs Popper as *Creating a Role* (1961). Later, from books already published in English and many other sources, I was able to glean his own pithy statements of his principal ideas and arrange them alphabetically to form a kind of dictionary of acting and the theatre. This we called *An Actor's Handbook* (1963).

Now that an increasing demand for *Stanislavski's Legacy* has shown that it transcends its special occasion, Stanislavski's publishers have urged me to search through the residue of his writings that have since been made available to find statements that fill out what we published in 1958 and add new dimensions. With Mrs. Popper's help again, we have added to Part Three and created a new section which we have subtitled, from a phrase in a letter Stanislavski wrote to Max Reinhardt, "Memories of the Past . . . Dreams of the Future." Although some of these new materials date from his last active years all are an integral part of an overall pattern of Stanislavski's purposes and accomplishments in the theatre and in life.

Stanislavski stands apart from many great artists in the profession of acting because, together with his personal talent—in itself very considerable and also a brilliant demonstration of his point of view of what acting could and should be—he combined a rare quality of self-discipline. With his quick and deep sensitiveness he was as "temperamental"—in all its senses—as any actor ever is, yet by preserving his immense self-control all his forces were channeled into working *with* his fellow actors in their common enterprise of forwarding the ideas of the playwright, whom he often, with profound insight, called the "poet."

Hence it was his life-long custom to delve into the "subtext" of any play, to find the essential meanings behind the printed words, really the inherent, when not always explicit, poetry of the author's inspiration, and then to translate that insight into the action of each character.

Thus his view when he was seventy is not essentially different from what it was when he was half that age, except that it was more far-reaching and more profound. He then had achieved a clearer realization that a life devoted to art is one of unremitting toil as well as one of high recompense in inner satisfactions.

Elizabeth Reynolds Hapgood

Petersham, Mass.

EDITOR'S FOREWORD

When Constantin Stanislavski died on August 8th, 1938 he was seventy-five and still in harness. I visited him in Moscow for two weeks in the Spring of 1937 and saw him work with actors from the Moscow Art Theatre on what later became a production of *Tartuffe,* I watched him rehearse young opera singers in *Madame Butterfly,* and I heard him discuss matters of art and theatre with a stream of visitors which included the ill-fated Vsevolod Meyerhold and also Prokofieff. At the same time he was continuing to write whenever he had a free moment. This aspect of his work is the concern of the present volume, for it is the tragedy of the actor that when his final curtain is rung down the image he has created vanishes. All that remains is the imprint the image has made on the minds and hearts of his audience and that too is ephemeral. Photographs can suggest something of an actor's power and versatility. The written word, if the actor happens to have the gift of verbal self-expression, provides a valuable and lasting record too, but the medium is so different from that of the acted word that often the impression gained by the reader is not altogether the one intended by the author.

Now twenty years after his death and thirty-five years after he appeared on the stage in America, Stanislavski is chiefly known as the author of two books which have been highly influential on the technique of acting in this country—*An Actor Prepares* and *Building A Character.* Yet from reading about Stanislavski's method many misinterpretations arose. Some actors tended to choose what appealed to them the most and did not make the effort to become what ideally might be called the "compleat actor" in a part, just as some teachers who claim to expound Stanislavski's method actually use only a fraction of his all-embracing technique. Weird tales have been current of exaggerated "feeling-your-part" actors who went into something akin to a trance, of others who said they were grand pianos or something else equally unlikely and even a "spool of purple thread" in Danny Kaye's amusing burlesque of Stanislavski—quite overlooking the fact that while training their imagination Stanislavski always dinned into his actors to say *"If* I were" Hamlet, or a tree, or even a grand piano, how would I react to the circumstances with which the playwright has seen fit to surround me, never to say "I am" this or that. The over-intellectual approach, the over-emotional approach, as well as the over-physical approach were all alike alien to Stanislavski in his search for truth. And let us add, the *truth in art,* for his emphasis was always on both art and life.

Stanislavski longed to record the fruit of his experiences and searchings; he actually planned the materials for a series of books of which only *My Life in Art* was actually published inside the Soviet Union during his lifetime (*An Actor Prepares* came out in the United States and in England nearly two full years before his death). At the same time he was distrustful of his ability to put what he had to say on paper; his medium was the acted word, for he was above all an actor working with actors. Besides, over the years he not only sought but also found fresh and more effective ways of drawing out of his fellow actors deeper and truer expressions of the characters they were portraying. With his characteristic honesty he was the first to recognize the shortcomings of any given approach, and on re-analyzing every facet of the problem he would reach out for a more satisfying solution.

Although Stanislavski was improving his technique up to the time of his death the changes in the last twenty years or more were not fundamental—they were largely a matter of shift in emphasis. The basic concept of what he often called "spiritual naturalism," because his idea was to breathe the spirit of life into each character portrayed, remained the granite foundation underlying his method.

The public which saw this technique in action when the Moscow Art Theatre visited Western Europe and America were made aware of the unique harmony an actor can achieve when all his creative forces (mind, heart, and will) are harnessed in the service of art and also the harmony of interplay among the characters in the performance. No productions of the Chekhov plays, for example, have ever rivalled those of the Art Theatre for comedy, tragedy and poignancy. Even Americans who understood not a word of Russian still remember those plays with emotion.

That visit, however, was thirty-five years ago and the Art Theatre was opened sixty years ago, in October 1898. In this multiple anniversary year it is fitting to publish this direct statement of Stanislavski's basic principles and aims, as revealed in many articles, talks, letters and other writings, which constitute a part of his legacy. I chose among these many materials items which seemed to me to concentrate on the essence and variety of his work. If some are extremely brief it is because occasionally in talking about other matters he chanced on a phrase that seemed to epitomize the deep implications of his findings. Longer pieces are published in their entirety because they throw a fresh light on the man and his method, or show him tackling a problem, like melodrama, about which he had not written in his books. The subjects are numerous because he sought constantly to widen the horizon of his actors and enrich their response to the variety of characters they would be called upon to play. In the process they enlarged their perception of themselves, of human beings and of life. The fiction writer has found in his method a key to unlock the active life of his characters; the salesman has found that by its means he can apprehend the inner workings of those he is seeking to convince. Here is meat for the public speaker, the teacher, the lawyer, the husband or wife, those whose aim is a better understanding of themselves and others, and above all for the actor who chooses to reach the heart of his character and through it the heart of the public.

Elizabeth Reynolds Hapgood

New York City
June 1958

Table of Contents

PART ONE

"In art you do not command,
you persuade...."

(Theatre) art creates the life of a human soul. We are called upon to interpret on the stage the life of contemporary man and his ideas. But we must not imitate our spectator, no, we must lead him up the rungs of a great ladder. Art must open his eyes to ideals, ideals created by the people.

(27 October 1928)

The laws of creativeness are immutable, binding on all, and they constitute a bond among artist actors of all nations. We must study these laws together, master them, work out for them a suitable psycho-technique of acting. . . . Let each nation, each people, reflect in its art its most subtle, national, human traits, and let each art preserve its own national colouring, tones, and distinctive features. And let this be the way to disclose the soul of each and every nation.

The Long-Hoped-for Child

... For me this theatre is a long-hoped-for, long-promised child. It is not for the sake of material gain that we have waited so long for it. No, it is the answer to our prayer for something to bring light and beauty into our humdrum lives. Let us be careful to appreciate what has fallen into our hands lest we shall soon be crying like the child who has broken his favourite toy. If we do not come to this enterprise with clean hands we shall defile it, disgrace ourselves and be scattered to the ends of Russia: some will go back to prosaic duties of everyday life, others, for the sake of keeping the wolf from the door, will profane their art in dirty, ramshackle theatres. Do not forget that if we break up with such a black mark against us we shall deserve to be laughed to scorn, because here we have undertaken something which is not a simple, private matter, but bears a public character.

Do not forget either that our goal is to bring enlightenment into the lives of the poor, to give them some aesthetic enjoyment amid the gloom in which they have been living. We are attempting to create the first thoughtful, high-minded, popular theatre—and to this great goal we are dedicating our lives.

Be careful not to crush this beautiful flower, else it will wilt and its petals fall.

A child is pure by nature. Human faults are grafted on him by his surroundings. Protect him from them and you will see that here among us he will develop into a being more ideal than we are, he will even cleanse us of our own unworthiness.

For the sake of such a purpose let us leave trivial matters at home, let us gather here in a common effort and not engage in petty squabbles and the settling of scores.... Let us be guided by the motto of "common work, friendly work," and then, believe me, for all of us the day will dawn

> When from the marble halls of the temple,
> Built by our own hands, the glad tidings
> Will resound and rend the heavy darkling clouds
> Hanging above our heads all this long wintertime,
> And pearls and diamonds from on high
> Will shower down on us...*

—from speech at first rehearsal of the Art Theatre (14 June 1898)

*From Gerhart Hauptmann's *The Sunken Bell*

What Shall We Learn?

Before we begin to study we must reach an agreement about what you wish to learn, otherwise we may run into a misunderstanding.

In the old-time theatres there were elements of the same fine and high-minded things that we too strive for, therefore we shall study the old carefully, conscientiously, so that we may learn to have a better perception of the new.

Let us not say that the theatre is a place of learning. No, the theatre stands for entertainment. We must not lose sight of this important factor. People should always come to the theatre to be entertained but once there, with the doors closed behind them, the lights lowered, we can pour into them anything we wish. For there is entertainment and entertainment.

Here you are, seated in the theatre. In front of you is fine scenery, sometimes a bit garish perhaps, sometimes something in more pleasing tones, depending on the action. Then there are splendid actors with arresting and fluent gestures, brilliant lights that rather dazzle you and leave you stunned, music too—all this is highly exciting, you are wrought up, your nerves are screwed to an ever increasing pitch. At the end you applaud, you cry "bravo!", dash onto the stage, embracing someone or other, plant a kiss here or there, get jostled about, etc. When you leave the theatre you are so agitated you cannot think of sleep, you must go to a restaurant with all your friends. At supper you review the spectacle and you remark on how good such and such an actress was. . . .

But the next day: what impression remains with you? Almost none, and a few days later you can really not be sure where it was that you applauded so warmly and the actors came out to take a bow. . . .

As for me I adore spectacles. I dote on vaudeville and farce when they are not off-colour.

But there is also another kind of theatre. You have come in and taken your seat as an onlooker, but the director of the play changes you into a participant in the life that is unfolding on the stage. Something has happened to you. You are carried away from your position as a mere onlooker. As soon as the curtain is drawn you say to yourself:

"I know this room, and there's Ivan Ivanovich, and there's my friend, Maria Petrovna. . . . Yes, I recognize all this. Now what happens next?" You are all ears. You look at the stage and you say:

"I believe it all, every bit of it. . . . That is my mother there. . . . I can tell . . ."

When the performance ends you are stirred, but in a different way now. You have no desire to applaud.

"How can I applaud my own mother? It feels rather strange."

The components of your excitement are such that they force you to concentrate, to turn your eyes inward. When you leave the theatre you do not wish to go to a restaurant. You are more drawn to some home or other, where you sit around the samovar and talk intimately about the problems of life, one's philosophic outlook, social problems.

And when your impressions have been with you overnight you find that vastly different things have remained in your mind. That other time you thought back and asked yourself with some concern: "Why did I dash onto the stage and kiss the tenor? To be sure he did sing well, but why did I have to kiss him? How silly. . . ."

But in the second instance your overnight impression has sunk much deeper into you: serious questions have been raised, they call for answers, you feel you did not take in all you should have,

6

you must return to the theatre. . . . The people you saw on the stage there, their lives, sufferings and joys wind themselves around your heart, they become part of you, these characters become your real friends.

"Let's go see the Prozorovs," or, "Let's go see Uncle Vanya." You are not going to see the *Three Sisters* or *Uncle Vanya* as plays, you are really going to call on old friends.

Older actors used to maintain that such close relationships were impossible between a regular stage and the audience, that it can be achieved only in a small compass. The Moscow Art Theatre rediscovered the means of establishing that relationship. It may well be that it does remain impossible in the Bolshoi (Opera) Theatre—there are limits in all things—yet I remember that when we were abroad we played in a Wiesbaden theatre which was really only slightly smaller than the Bolshoi, and that only goes to prove that our kind of art can be conveyed also to a very large crowd of people.

So we have first a theatre which is a spectacle, an entertainment for eye and ear, and that is its ultimate aim.

In the second kind of theatre the effect on your eyes and ears is only a means to penetrate the soul of the audience.

The first theatre is under the necessity of cajoling the eye or else dazzling it and in any case emotions must be torn to tatters. The actor knows this and as a result there are no lengths to which he will not go. If his temperament is insufficient he will scream, he will suddenly race his lines, he will underscore every syllable, he will intone.

Just think what the power is of this institution that we call the theatre! You can raise a crowd to a state of ecstasy, and you can agitate them, wind them around, you can mix them all up together, or on the contrary you can make them sit motionless and accept anything you choose to inculcate, you can appeal to the herd instinct in them, etc.

Painting, music and the other arts which individually exercise

7

an immediate appeal to the human soul, are united in one whole in the theatre and that is what so reinforces its power.

I well remember what Leo Tolstoy, whom I met for the first time at Nikolai Davydov's (the great actor), said on this subject: "The theatre is the most powerful pulpit of our times." It is more powerful than school or church. Before you go to school you must have the desire to go instilled in you. Everyone goes voluntarily to the theatre because everyone wishes to be entertained. In school you must learn how to remember what is taught you, but in the theatre what is poured into you remains with you of its own accord.

The theatre is the most powerful weapon of all, but like all weapons it has a double potential: it can bring great good and it may cause great harm.

Now if we ask ourselves: What are our theatres doing for people, what will the reply be? I am speaking now of all theatres, beginning with that of Duse, Chaliapine and other great artists and ending with that of Saburov, the Hermitage Variety Theatre and anything else that goes under the name of theatre.

The evil that a bad book can do is not to be compared with that which the theatre can inflict, neither as to the power of the infection nor as to the ease with which the evil spreads among the masses. And yet the theatre as an institution contains elements of popular education, primarily aesthetic education, for the masses.

This then is the dread power which you contemplate taking into your hands, this is the responsibility which will be laid upon you to handle this power in the right way.

—Speech to students, assistants and actors of the Moscow
Art Theatre Second Company ("Filial") (March 1911)

The Hard Job of Being an Actor

Remember that my objective is to teach you the hard work of an actor and director of plays—it is not to provide you with a pleasant pastime on the stage. There are other theatres, teachers and methods for that. The work of an actor and director, as we understand it here, is a painful process, not merely some abstract "joy of creativeness" that one hears so much empty talk about from the ignoramuses in art. Our work gives us joy when we undertake it. This is the joy of being conscious that we may, that we have the right, that we have been permitted to engage in the work we love—work to which we have dedicated our lives. And our work gives us joy when we see that having fulfilled our task, put on a performance, played a role, we have contributed something worthwhile to our audience, communicated to it something necessary, important to its life, for its development. In short I come back to the ideas of Gogol and Shchepkin about the theatre, words you have already heard many times from me and probably will hear more than once again.

Nevertheless the whole process of an actor's and director's work—including his performance—is one that requires enormous self-mastery and often also great physical endurance. This work cannot be replaced by means of general words and moods.

The thing which lies at the base of an actor's or director's creativeness is work, and not moods or any other popular slogans such as "flights," "down beats," "triumphs."

To the ordinary man in the street the most "joyous" jobs might be the dance of the prima ballerina in *Don Quixote* or *Swan Lake*. He does not know how much physical effort, concentrated attention, sheer work Madame Geltzer had to put into the preparation

9

of her famous "pas de deux" in those ballets, or what she looks like when she is in her dressing room after the dance is over. Perspiration pours from her and in her heart she reproaches herself for any slightest shading she did not perform perfectly.

That is true of dancing. Why should it be easier in drama or comedy? Yes, the "joy of creativeness" exists and it falls to the lot of true artists after they have done a tremendous piece of work in any chosen and beloved field of work in which they reach the goals they have set themselves.

But the artist is not worth his salt who impersonates the "joy of creativeness," waves his brushes around in front of his easel, pretending he is "painting" with such "ecstasy" (that's another popular word among the modernists). He is profaning his art at such times. He is not trying to reproduce life on his canvas, life in its infinite manifestations, trying to catch the fleeting feeling or thought on the face of his model. All he is trying to do is become her lover.

The same is true of an actor on the stage. When you act as you did recently the "joy of creativeness" instead of the subject and ideas of the play, you are just flirting with the public like actor-prostitutes. Not that! Never! Leave this to the decadent artist, the futurist, cubist! The great Russian actors, painters and writers did not play fast and loose with life, rather they tried to show its revolting and its inspiring sides in order to *educate* their public.

Do not be afraid of that word in art.

I have talked at length to you on the general subject of our theatre art because I not only want you to know how to play your parts better but also to learn how to *train* yourselves to become real artists. Whatever I have achieved has been at the price of tremendous work, of years wasted in mistakes and deviations from the real line of art. I am turning over to you everything I have learned, all my experience, in order to keep you from making the same mistakes. You will have three times as much opportunity to push our art ahead if you will follow me, choose to follow the path which I point out to you.

You are a new generation, come into the theatre since the revolution. I want you to learn again in practice what is called the "Stanislavski Method." There is no "method" as yet. There are a number of propositions and exercises which I propose to actors to carry out: they are to work on themselves, train themselves to become master artists. What are the basic propositions of my "method"?

The *first* is this: There are no formulas in it on how to become a great actor, or how to play this or that part. The "method" is made up of steps towards the true creative state of an actor on the stage. When it is true it is the usual, normal state of a person in real life.

But to achieve that normal living state on stage is very difficult for an actor. In order to do it: (a) he has to be physically free, in control of free muscles; (b) his attention must be infinitely alert; (c) he must be able to listen and observe on the stage as he would in real life, that is to say to be in contact with the person playing opposite him; (d) he must believe in everything that is happening on the stage that is related to the play.

To accomplish this I shall propose a number of exercises.... They train these absolutely necessary qualities in actors. They shall be done every day the way a singer vocalizes or a pianist does his finger exercises.

The *second* proposition of the "method" is: A true inner creative state on the stage makes it possible for an actor to execute the actions necessary for him to take in accordance with the terms of the play, whether inner psychological actions or external, physical ones. I divide them this way arbitrarily to make it easier to explain them to you in rehearsal. Actually in each physical act there is an inner psychological motive which impels physical action, as in every psychological inner action there is also physical action, which expresses its psychic nature.

The union of these two actions results in organic action on the stage.

That action then is determined by the subject of the play, its idea, the character of a certain part and the circumstances set up by the playwright.

In order to make it easier for you as an actor to take action on the stage, put yourself first of all in the circumstances proposed by the playwright for the character you are playing. Ask yourself: what would I do *if* the same thing should happen to me as it does in the play to the character I am playing? I call *if* jokingly a "magic" word because it does so much to help an actor get into action. Having learned to take action for yourself, then determine what difference there is between your own actions and those of your character in the play. Find out all the reasons which justify the actions of your character and then act without reflecting about just where your "own" actions end and "his" begin. The one and the other will merge of their own accord if you have followed the procedure I have indicated to you.

The *third* proposition of the system: True organic action (inner-plus-external, psychological-plus-physical) is bound to give rise to sincere feelings. This is especially true if the actor can in addition find some attractive "bait," as we saw in rehearsal.

Therefore the summing up is:

A *true inner creative state* on the stage, *action* and *feeling* result in *natural life* on the stage in the form of one of the characters. It is by this means that you will come closest to what we call "metamorphosis," always providing of course that you have properly understood the play, its idea, its subject and plot, and have shaped inside yourself the character of one of the dramatis personae.

(6 October 1924)

Types of Actors

In the world of dramatic art it has long been customary to divide actors into a number of categories: good, villainous, gay, suffering, bright, stupid, etc. This division of actors into groups is called type-casting.

Therefore there are the following types: tragedians (men and women), dramatic lovers, second-line lovers and dandies, dramatic and comic old men and women, noble fathers, character parts, moralists, comedians and simple-minded creatures, farce comedians, vaudeville lovers, *grandes dames,* dramatic and comic ingénues, vaudeville actors who can sing and play second- and third-rate parts.

More recently new subdivisions have been introduced. There have appeared shirt-sleeve lovers and earthy actresses, wicked and villainous characters, nervous roles (neurasthenic), roles with tears, society and non-society roles, costume roles, burlesque players, cocottes, Ibsen parts, brainy parts, special roles in plays by Ostrovski, Hauptmann, Dostoyevski, etc.

Here are some of the conversations I have overheard:

"What kind of roles do you play?"

"Country teachers, tear jerkers."

"And you?"

"I play city crooks and men about town."

Still others reply:

"I play Gothic monsters and costume heroes."

The fourth, fifth, sixth groups answer:

"I play old men, officials with a nervous twitch."

"I play neurasthenic Hauptmann roles."

"I love the Ibsen ones, with a touch of mist about them."

As you see this typing of actors has been broken up into authors and even individual parts. We now have specialists in such parts as Tsar Fyodor or Hannele.

Theatre habits have made those divisions by type legitimate. For instance it is not being a good fellow if you take the type part away from someone else. With the exception of guest actors, who are not subject to any laws, and some individual actors who make a point of having only the good parts, all the rest are placed in restrictive and small pigeonholes, which keep them well inside their own categories. That is why a tragic actor is eternally condemned to be wrapped in a costume cape, and suffer and die on stage. The simple-minded fellow has to be forever amazed at the complication of affairs into which the author has plunged him, the ingénue will have to play being naïve all her life, she will skip around, clap her hands, and babble sweetly, and the poor circus clowns always have to make people laugh at their deformities.

Can one under such conditions ask for variety? And isn't it natural that roles eternally handed down will be played in an eternally fixed method? What is so surprising in the fact that actors who spend three quarters of the day in the theatre or learning their parts, should let these methods permeate their flesh and blood? These methods transform an actor, who is to begin with a real human being, into what the public sees every day in the theatre.

That is why even off stage the tragedian looks morose, the comedian cracks jokes, the ingénue goes around being charming, the tragic actress is forever suffering and the dandy talks trivialities.

That is why these unfortunate actors are so monotonous, unnatural and boring both on stage and off. Since art to them is no longer a creative goal it is converted into heavy routine, and if it were not for the bohemian life of these hard-working people, which contains some attractive elements of freedom, albeit rather unbridled, they would scarcely be able to breathe. Alas, the actors' bohemian life is attractive but also poisonous.

This is what Tolstoy has to say in his novel *Resurrection:*
"One of the most usual and widespread superstitions is that every
person possesses only his own clear-cut qualities, that a man is
good, evil, intelligent, stupid, energetic, apathetic, etc. People are
not like that. We can say of a man that he is more good than
bad, more often intelligent than stupid, more often energetic than
apathetic, or vice versa: but it will be untrue if we say of one man
that he is good or clever, and of another that he is bad or stupid.
Yet we are always dividing people. And that is not right. People
are like rivers: they all contain the same water everywhere, yet
each river at times will be narrow, swift, broad, smooth-flowing,
clear, cold, muddy, warm. So it is with people. Each man carries
within himself the germs of all human qualities, and sometimes
he manifests the one or the other and is often quite unlike himself, while still remaining the very same person. In some people
these changes are especially abrupt ... they occur because of some
physical or spiritual reason."

My feeling is that the division of actors into types is furthered
by the unfavourable conditions prevailing in theatres—the haste
with which work is done and the pressure to lighten and speed it
up for the actors.

You will remember how the craftsmen work in the cottage
industries: one man is good and quick at carving legs, another
arms, a third does the backs, a fourth assembles and glues the
whole together, so that in the end you have a craftmade chair.
As a result of constant practice and adaptability to narrowly
defined specialization these craftsmen acquire speed with a minimum of labour. Is this not true also of the practices in theatrical
enterprises which are aimed at material rather than artistic goals?
Their name is legion. Why there are actors in those theatres who
can play nothing but comic oldsters, stupid youngsters, while
others do not know how to do anything except cry or laugh well.
The directors of the plays paste them together and get a miserable
production that does not survive more than two or three perform-

ances. Yet under that system they succeed in staging a hundred or more plays in a season.

Is it possible to require of actors fresh observation, a variety of types, varying styles of acting, a searching for new forms in order to express the individuality of the playwright, in short, is it possible to expect creative work on their part when a play is put on with from one to ten rehearsals at most? Finally, can an actor possess the imagination to create from fifty to a hundred roles in a year? Yet that is what a provincial actor is often required to do. Is it astounding then that these unfortunate and hard-pressed actors have recourse first to craft and then to mass production methods in preparing their parts? What happens is a division of labour with each actor having his own specialized field of endeavour. In other words the actors are type-cast and the productions are tradition bound and use certain fixed methods of acting.

Type-casting may speed up an actor's work and loud declaiming will mask its poor quality.

These are just a few of the many conditions which bolster the mistaken custom of dividing actors into types.

The typing of actors moderates their greed for fat parts, and effects something of a fair division of work among them. Everyone knows that jealousy of another's success and good roles are the two major apples of discord among actors. Type-casting has a slightly beneficent effect in matters of jealousy. Only in rare instances does the tragedian envy the comedian, whereas it is often the case that two actors of the same type cannot coexist comfortably in the same company.

The most ardent partisans of the custom of type-casting are the poorly endowed actors, whose range is not broad but rather one-sided. Such gifts as they have are somehow made to do for narrowly circumscribed types, but they are unlikely to be sufficient to meet any wider demands.

Anyone who has even the most rudimentary external or inner gifts and experience on the stage can find one or two, even five roles that he can play reasonably well if the main qualities of these parts are suited to his own nature. All he has to do is to collect about ten such parts, differentiating them by changing his clothes, beards and wigs, and then he can qualify as an actor of such and such a type.

That is why we often see people of both sexes, who have been failures in other lines and who crave an independent and free profession, probing their way into the theatre, and in a year or so they become actors without exceptional talents, preparation for work or study. You could not achieve this result in any other art, but the theatre, so they think, is open at once to any talent, and who does not think he has some? Therefore a man of fair stature and loud voice will become either a tragedian or peasant lover. A handsome young man with a certain dash will become the youthful lover—if he is absolutely without talent he will play the second-string lover. When this latter makes an effort, acquires a sufficient wardrobe and a way with women, he will become a dandy and high class villain. The man who can tell funny stories will be the comedian; if he is ugly he will be the clown-comedian. An older man without a spark of temperament will get the part of the moralist. Anyone who has been a merchant in real life will take the part of a merchant in Ostrovski's plays. A woman who is hysterical by nature will become a dramatic actress. One who is neurasthenic in ordinary life will be the same on the stage. A beautiful woman without any talent is at once a *grande dame* and a *grande coquette*. A young girl who is of slight build and gay is, of course, the *ingénue*. If she is taller and rather a bore—the *ingénue dramatique*. If she has a voice she will sing in vaudeville. The very reckless type of girl will go into burlesque, and so on and so forth.

In brief all you need is a modicum of external, inner, even morbid qualities to become an actor of a given type.

A true artist is of a different opinion: he does not hold with type-casting, he plays all kinds of parts except those that go

17

against the grain with him by reason of his convictions or taste. For instance when he was forty Rossi played a magnificent young Romeo, and when she was fifty and fat Madame Judique was enchanting in the parts of eighteen-year-old girls. These same actors were also applauded in very much older parts, with this difference—that the younger roles were somewhat less suited to their external appearance.

To my way of thinking there can be only one type of actor—the character actor. Any role that does not include a real characterization will be poor, not lifelike, and the actor who cannot convey the character of the roles he plays is a poor and monotonous actor.

As a matter of fact, there is no person on earth who does not possess his own individual character. Even the most colourless person is distinguished by his character of utter lack of colour.

That is why I propose for actors a complete inner and external metamorphosis.

Perhaps this is an unattainable goal, as unattainable as any ideal, yet the ardent pursuit of it will, to a person of talent, open new horizons, a wide field for creativeness, an unfailing source of work, observation, study of life and people and consequently, of self-education and self-improvement.

Perhaps it is beyond the powers of those who are not gifted. Nevertheless the pursuit of this goal is bound to precipitate a fight against whatever is sheer routine and it will overcome this worst enemy of art.

When actors will be forced to look to life for materials out of which to create their parts, and not among dusty, outworn, threadbare theatrical collections of images, then they will be divided into only two categories: good actors and bad actors. And the costume actors in their blouses, their frock coats and other trappings from their five-role repertories will vanish into oblivion.

Such sweeping qualifications to be demanded from an actor should really be of service to the unfortunate young men and women who, like butterflies, singe their wings on the footlights. They will finally realize that dramatic art, like all other arts which hold a mirror up to life, requires talent, study and self-perfection. And realizing this they will approach the stage more cautiously.

Perhaps then too all the falseness which has built itself such a comfortable nest backstage will disappear. God willing we shall also see the end of loud talk about all sorts of rules in art, which on the lips of actors without talent, impress the trusting public.

"Dreams! Carried away by dreams! You ascribe too much significance to the small doings of type actors in the theatre"— that is what many will think when they read these pages.

That well may be. But let it stir discussion, criticism, argument, let people search for other and truer methods of driving artistic and other falseness from the theatre, of replacing them with artistic truth, of improving the ground for the broad and not the narrowly circumscribed development of talent, of making the public search in the theatre for a reflection of real, not papier-maché life.

There is only one thing about which I have no doubt—that to be able to transform one's self physically and spiritually is the first and principle object of acting art.

When the public comes to know actors of this sort it will quickly change its ways, it will value creativeness on the stage instead of rubber-stamp art.

That is sufficient to raise the standard of the theatre, the directors of plays, the actors and everyone else involved with the stage. This is the very best filtre which will protect the theatre from being flooded with mediocrities.

(Undated)

On Being Truthful in Acting

What does it really mean to be truthful on the stage? ... Does it mean that you conduct yourself as you do in ordinary life? Not at all. Truthfulness in those terms would be sheer triviality. There is the same difference between artistic and inartistic truth as exists between a painting and a photograph: the latter reproduces everything, the former only what is essential; to put the essential on canvas requires the talent of a painter.

(1905)

Acting Looks Easy

The work of an actor looks easy because it is agreeable and the results are attractive. To possess power over a crowd of people, adulation, success, ovations, popularity, fame—those are the enticing elements in the career of an actor.

Alas, it is only for the chosen few that such beautiful prospects are opened. The life of the majority of actors is difficult, drab and unlovely. The public is not aware of this life because it is forever hidden behind a gaily painted curtain.

This is now a good moment to lift a corner of this curtain and look into the mysterious region of backstage which is so brilliantly lighted at night and so dark in the daytime. Very few stages are well constructed so I shall tell you what the majority of them are like.

Picture a large shed, cluttered up with dusty pieces of old settings, and roofed over with rusty iron. The place is always dirty and badly heated. They say that dirt is an inevitable condition of a stage and that heating is superfluous because the public warms up the building by its breath and body heat.

Both the dirt and the heat are brought into the theatre gratuitously. Besides, when the theatre was lighted by gas, that generated a considerable amount of warmth which was not supplemented by other heating means. The whole trick was how to retain the heat thus generated. That, however, was very simple: all sources of ventilation were carefully nailed up wherever possible: doors, windows, ventilating sections of windows. This prevented the heat from escaping and the cold from coming in.

In such theatres the actors' dressing rooms are usually partitioned off in some dark corner of the stage with thin wooden walls, rather like box stalls.

Daylight is recognized as being not only superfluous in the dressing rooms but even harmful because it interferes with putting on make-up. For reasons of economy and fire hazards it is forbidden to turn on the gas lights in these dark dressing rooms during the daytime, and in the evening by contrast they burn brightly and give off a great deal of heat.

The dressing rooms are not at all furnished. They drag in odd bits of furniture which have gone out of use either on the stage or the clean parts of the theatre—a chair with a bent-in leg or the seat out but still carrying a plate with its number on it from the auditorium. Or perhaps there's a little sofa in the corner, with all its legs off, therefore unfit for use on the stage. Hanging space is provided by nails driven into the walls. An old slab of wood, scribbled over with names, bad verse and caricatures, serves as a make-up table. That, more or less, is the way the backstage still looks in, unfortunately, the greater number of theatres.

The habits, ethical standards and way of life of people correspond to the conditions in which they live.

Most actors are obliged by necessity to accustom themselves to spending three quarters of their lives in a bare, dirty shed. The remainder which is spent outside the theatre does not have the power to displace the habits formed backstage, so that the actor's way of life there is the same in his own home.

To be the inhabitant of a dingy shed in the daytime and be transformed into a king in the evening, to combine the realities of day with the embodiment of the poetry of art in the evening— such is the contradiction inherent in an actor's life, such are the contrasts which throw him off his balance and create a very special kind of existence for him—an existence which destroys his organism, shatters his nervous system and ages him prematurely.

I do not know of any other cultured existence which would reconcile itself to such conditions which are like those of an unskilled labourer or life in a basement. Who, for instance, would be willing for the sake of his work to sit for half of his life in a small cramped space, with his feet down in the cold and damp, and his head surrounded by scorching gas lamps? This is the torture voluntarily suffered by any prompter in the theatre and for it he receives a pittance. Everyone knows that this friend of actors will inevitably suffer fierce rheumatism, but no one does anything about improving his inhuman conditions of work. And if a prompter because he has caught cold takes a drink to warm himself he is punished as if he were an habitual drunkard. Who is willing, after the excitement of five hours' work in the stifling atmosphere of the stage, to take a rest in an unheated dressing room or put on his clothes which are coated with frost and which he must almost tear off the frozen wall?

Many actors are really risking their lives in these conditions. Nor is that all: actors are often arrayed in tights and cloaks or the costumes of peoples who inhabit the tropics and obliged to spend an entire evening in the unheated structure which is the stage.

How can one explain this inhuman attitude towards people who are dedicated to their art and why do they tolerate such exploitation of their work?

The love which an actor has for his art obliges him patiently to bear all deprivations. Such sacrifices are made not only by the actors who receive the laurels and ovations down in front by the footlights but also even by the unnoticed co-workers, the actors who speak only a phrase or two during the whole performance.

The work of these actors is hard and the results are not always glamorous. Actors work not only during the day but also during the hours when other people are resting.

The actor exchanges the light of the morning sun and fresh air for the dark of night and the dark painful life in the wings, and his rest he exchanges for the blinding brilliance of the footlights.

At midnight when others are asleep and gather strength for the next day, the exhausted actor is still experiencing the last agonies of the hero of the play and for a long time after the performance is over the light will still be burning in his room—the only witness to the doubts, disappointments and tortures of a creative artist. In the morning he wakes up when other people do and hurries off to rehearsal.

A stern art does not take into consideration the rest which is an absolute need of an artist. A long-drawn-out rehearsal often robs him of the possibility of getting a hot dinner. It would have been a modest meal in any case because when he eats anything the actor must bear in mind not to impair his voice for his evening performance.

We have seen a loving couple immediately after their marriage ceremony slip off their wedding clothes to put on their stage costumes. I have seen a worried husband severely reprimanded for arriving late for a performance after he had been detained at home by a serious operation just performed on his wife; he had not even stayed to the end of it but had rushed to the theatre, exchanging his duty as a family man for his obligation as an actor. We have seen a father, broken with grief, entertain an audience and then run into the wings to weep over news that a member of his family is dying. We have seen an audience whistle down a singer who missed his high note: He was singing on the day he buried his wife.

Think what an effort of memory is involved to learn in one night a five-act part in verse which you were given the previous evening! What energy you must muster to thread your way through the intricacies of a whole production, and what excitement you must experience, in order to be able to appear without preparation before an audience and yet keep the fact of your hasty work a secret from them.

The public thinks that on such occasions actors do things much more simply, that they do not even look at their lines but walk on the stage without having read the play. There is even an anecdote about one actor who, while taking off his make-up after a performance and pulling off his whiskers, exclaimed: "It's a good play, I'll have to read it." Perhaps there are actors who do such things, who have lost their faith and dried up inside—yet I know fine old actors who work late into the night on their parts, who tremble before they make their entrances and after the performance is over, with tears and anguish, cry out in the dressing room: "How can they ruin such a marvellous play, how can one make people trample their ideals underfoot and present them in that state to an audience?"

These anguished cries of artists are heard every day and from one end of the globe to the other, nor are they without effect on the health of the artists.

They work nearly all day and all year round. They prepare and play often as many as a hundred and fifty new roles in a year, and many are good actors who contribute their full share for the good of their public.

What is the end reward of all this superhuman work? It is rather sorry: a series of bitter disappointments. Complete lack of material security, exhaustion, often long journeys back home, even on foot along the railroad tracks "from Kerch to Vologda." [A quotation from an Ostrovski play meaning practically from one end of Russia to the other.—Ed.]

Fortunately, some improvements in the conditions under which actors must labour have now been undertaken. Theatre societies, individual producers, wealthy patrons are making efforts in this direction and some old veterans of the stage have shelters to which they can repair in institutions set up especially for them. God willing, this good work will grow and prosper, but we must be thinking about the young and healthy actors, we must protect them from premature old age. That should not be too difficult to achieve.

Perhaps the present movement to found a sanatorium near some mineral springs in the Caucasus will offer the possibility for needy and exhausted actors to enjoy the gifts nature has lavished on that country for the benefit of suffering humanity.

Please help actors speed this excellent undertaking and remember how responsive they themselves are to the needs of society, gladly giving their services for all sorts of benefit performances.

Let these actors who work all through the year have a chance to keep up their spirits by looking forward to a period of rest. In the heavy turmoil of the winter season let them be comforted by the words of Chekhov in *Uncle Vanya*: "We shall rest! We shall rest!"

(Circa 1905)

An Actor Is a Teacher of Beauty and Truth – Letter to a Young Student

I have not written you until now because I was very busy. I have had rehearsals from twelve to five, by six-thirty it was time to put on my make-up and the play lasted until midnight. That is how I spend each day—do not imagine that theatrical laurels are to be won without real work.

Your first letter pleased me very much with its feeling of youthful sincerity and although my correspondence is very heavy I decided I must reply to it because, you see, I once lived through all the emotions which now are affecting you. I feel sure that I can offer you some good and sensible counsel. But I shall not conceal from you the fact that I did not like your second letter. There was an air about it of offended petty pride. Such phrases as: "If I'm asking something I shouldn't, I shan't insist," "No doubt I'll manage by myself anyhow," etc.—all this suggests that you, so very young as you are, feel your *amour-propre* is impinged upon. If that is really the case then I must tell you it is very dangerous ground for a future actor. I should prefer to overlook these words which otherwise would prevent me from speaking to you quite frankly.

Do you know why I gave up my personal business affairs and went into the theatre? Because the theatre is the most powerful pulpit there is, far more potent in its influence than books or newspapers. This pulpit has fallen into the hands of the dregs of human society and they have corrupted it. My goal is, to the extent of my powers, to cleanse my group of actors from being ignoramuses, half-baked people and exploiters. My goal is, to the extent of my powers, to make clear to the present generation that an actor is a teacher of beauty and truth. For this an actor must rise above the mob by virtue of his talent or cultivation or other capacities. An actor must be above all a cultured person, be able to pull himself up to the level of the geniuses of literature.

That is why we do not, to my way of thinking, have any real actors. Out of a thousand people of no gifts, drunkards, half-baked creatures who call themselves actors we must reject 999, choosing only one who is worthy of the name of actor. My company is made up of university men, technicians, people who have completed their education—and it is in this fact that you will find the power of our theatre.

A love of the theatre has been born in you. Begin now to make sacrifices to it, by which I mean that service to art consists in the ability to make selfless sacrifices to it. Study on and when you will be a literate and well-rounded person come to me and then my work will appeal to you. With me and my companions you will prepare to follow a thorny, difficult and painful path, and you will forget all about fame and you will love your work. Yet all of this is, of course, premised on your having talent.... Still talent is not enough, especially in the theatre of the twentieth century—new Ibsens, raised to a second power as to philosophic and social content, will provide the repertory of this coming theatre and such authors can be performed only by cultivated people. We have done with provincial ranters and contortionists and soon, God grant, the time will come when by law illiterate people will be excluded from service on the stage—indeed a congress of actors is now working towards that end. To check what I have said read *The Master Builder* of Ibsen, his *Hedda Gabler,* and decide for yourself how much longer you will have to pursue your studies in order to understand this world genius. These are just the blossoms, the fruits are yet to come. So continue to study and I shall be glad to accept you as a helper, but if you remain untutored I shall consider you an enemy of the theatre and I shall train all my guns against you. Your well wisher,

C. Stanislavski.

Forgive the bad writing and lapses. I have no time for corrections as I am writing this between the acts. (11 March 1901)

Lively Art

It is a good thing in art when people are really alive, when they make an effort to reach a given point, when they repulse something, struggle for something, quarrel over something, overcome obstacles or are even anguished. Battle brings victory and conquest. The worst is when all is quiescent in art, all in order, definite, legitimate, when there is no need of argument, struggle, when there are no defeats, hence no victories either. Art and artists must move forward or else they will move backward.

(June 1938)

How to Talk to Actors

You cannot talk to actors in dry, scientific language, and indeed I am myself not a man of science so I could not do it in any case.

My task is to talk to the actor in his own language, not in order to philosophize about art...but rather to open up for him in simple form the ways of a psycho-technique which is a practical necessity to him; this he must have above all in the inner realm of the artistic and emotional realization of a role as well as in his physical incarnation of it. . . .

The terminology I use...was not invented by me, I took it from the practical expressions of student actors; I defined their creative feelings in verbal terms. These are valuable in that they are close to a beginner's comprehension.

Do not look for any scholarly or scientific derivations. We in the theatre have our own lexicon, our actors' jargon which has been wrought out of life. We do use, to be sure, certain scientific terms too, as for example "the subconscious," "intuition," but we take them in their everyday, simplest connotation and not in any philosophical sense. It is not our fault that scholars have neglected the field of theatre art, that we have not been provided with terms for our practical work. In this predicament we have to extricate ourselves by forging our own home-made tools.

—from the introduction to the first Russian edition of *An Actor Prepares* (1938)

Talks with Singers to Be Trained as Actors

When life brings people together in the field of art it is not a fortuitous happening; in some it is because their hearts are aflame with a single desire, to share their experiences, and then to move forward; they cannot stand still, their inner resources are growing in power, they are seeking new outlets in action for their creative forces.

Perhaps you will ask: If art is an individual and once-trodden path for each artist, can one form a studio where many are taught? In our studio we shall see that each human being carries his own creative faculties in himself, and although his inner fire will not burn with the same ardour as that of another, still there are many degrees of work and many problems which are common to all of them because their goal is the same: to discover the nature of the forces they harbour within themselves.

The actor who merely observes life around him from the sidelines, experiences its joys and sorrows without ever seeking to probe into their complex origins, or ever looking beyond them to the grandeur of life's events, the inherent drama, the high heroism—that actor is lacking in true creative instinct.

Learn to see, hear, love life—learn to carry this over into art, use it to fill out the image you create for yourself of a character you are to play.

(1918)

31

Talks with Opera and Acting Students

You are preparing to participate in a collective undertaking. What does that mean? It means that you must be welded into one collective whole and learn as a group to care for your common work. And to learn how to do this means that you will be re-educated both as a person and as an actor.

The painters or the poets sit at home, or in their studios, they are not dependent on anyone and they can work whenever they choose. In your work you are bound up with a whole group, and you are obliged to do your work before an audience of thousands, and not at a time you choose, but at the exact hour announced on the billboards.... Do you comprehend the entire responsibility you are shouldering, and the necessity of training yourselves under a special creative discipline? That is what we are preparing you for and why we are graduating you from our school, not as individuals (which I consider has no purpose) but in whole groups.

The success of an actor does not depend only on himself, but also on his partner who may do a good or bad job of holding up his end during creative moments. And an opera singer is, in addition, dependent on the conductor. Also the backstage atmosphere exercises considerable influence on your work. An actor is dependent on his dresser, on the electrician. This is the special character of collective creativeness to which you must accustom yourselves and which you must come to understand. You depend on your fellow students as they depend on you. Collective art can be created only in an atmosphere of friendliness and mutual help. Interest in your relationships with your fellow students is interest in your common work. An actor works under conditions of nervous intensity. He is peculiarly over-anxious and ambitious. You must learn to hold yourselves in check, to be patient and friendly with your associates; these are the conditions of working in a joint enterprise.

I know many theatres which have ceased to be joint enterprises, and have turned into collections of mutually hostile people. They used to be an amiable collective, but with the years they have lost their cohesion and broken up.

The problem of collective enterprise is important and complex. You must not only recognize it but feel it very deeply. Each one of you must weigh your conduct from the point of view of the good of the whole. You must speak only of what will do no harm to the theatre.

If you are unable to grasp the peculiar conditions of collective creativeness and cannot allow yourselves to be absorbed in it, your group will lose its common goal and will become nothing more than a hatching ground for all sorts of horrid things.

We must be assured that all your energy will be directed towards keeping our common cause intact, and your instructors for their part will be thinking of how to set up a programme of instructions calculated to train you for collective creativeness.

Learn how to love art in yourselves, not yourselves in art. If you undertake to exploit art it will betray you: art is very vindictive. I repeat: love art in yourselves, not yourselves in art—that should be your guiding thread. The theatre does not exist for you, you exist for the theatre.

There is no higher satisfaction than working in the field of art, but it requires sacrifice.

You will have to acquire an iron—and I am not afraid to say—a soldier's discipline. An actor who, when he enters the theatre, does not feel a slight tremor pass through him at the thought that here, nearby, is the stage, will never be a true actor. If you have this deep inner discipline, which stems from respect for your work, the atmosphere backstage will be peculiarly helpful to creativeness. And that atmosphere is always transmitted in some strange manner to the auditorium. The public always senses what is going on backstage, and is affected by it. How this happens I do not know. It is a secret. If I make the remark that you make too much noise with your chairs when you sit down, note that this too has a bearing on the artistic discipline I am trying to instill in you.

Stand up, but don't make any noise.

Move the chairs so that no noise will be heard....

For every sound there will be—a penalty!

Now learn this elementary discipline from the word go, and begin by moving those chairs without a sound.

Once the widow of Richard Wagner took me backstage (during a performance of *The Flying Dutchman*). In the space of one minute the ship had to be removed, and in its place were put the women with their spinning wheels—and all without a single sound.

On another occasion a table laden with crystalware had to be removed instantly from the stage. What happened was that each actor took his share and carried it off. This was done in absolute silence, there was not a clink of glass to be heard.

Discipline is not only necessary for the maintenance of order, without which collective creative work is impossible, but also for artistic purposes. It provides the needed atmosphere.

You must study systematically to gain control of your art. That control is what, as a rule, an actor lacks. An opera singer must always care for his instrument, his voice, or he cannot sing. But the actor reasons thus: "I know how to walk, I know how to talk," so he goes on the stage. Yet as a matter of fact an actor needs perhaps even more training than an opera singer. An opera singer

comes to this school with his art of singing already in his possession, it is only the acting he needs to learn.

Now a violinist has to care every single day for his instrument.
When I was in America I went to an evening party where the
famous violinist Jascha Heifetz was present. At the very high
point of the evening, when we were sitting down to dinner
Heifetz suddenly disappeared. Later on he appeared again. It
seemed that he had a concert scheduled for the next day. He had
driven home to move his violin into a cabinet with a certain tem-
perature and degree of humidity. No one but he would do a thing
like this.

I remember when Sarah Bernhardt came to play here. One of
her legs had been amputated, but she continued to act L'Aiglon
in the Rostand play; it was an amazing piece of technical perfection. But what did it cost her? Every day she sang, exercised her
voice in diction, fenced with trainers she took along on her journeys. She was in the midst of these exercises when I went in to
see her.

You have an instrument of expression. You must perfect it and
care for it. One cannot play Beethoven off key, or on an instrument which is out of tune. Your instrument must be well tuned so
that you can render on it all the shadings of your emotions.

Even though you feel perfectly well, if your body does not
correspond to your emotions, if your voice does not carry or your
hands are cramped, people will only laugh at your feelings.

Think of a man who is deaf and dumb. He wants to make a
declaration of love and all he can do is make incoherent sounds.
Can you understand him? Imagine his anguish.

The deeper your feelings, the more complicated the pattern of
your emotions, the greater should be the expressive capacity of
your body. Let your teachers find out which muscles you need to
develop, find out what your particular weaknesses are. Work on
these exercises and keep them up for years. Develop your hands

and fingers. The fingers are the eyes of the body, you can express anything with them.

Train yourselves so that your muscles believe in the rightness of your movements, let them seek the way to perform. Keep at this for years.

What does one mean by control of the body? It is not enough to know how to place your feet when you walk, etc. You must train yourselves to live, walk, talk while an inner supervisor controls all your movements. This supervisor works without regard for your will, and he sees to it that your external conduct is right.

Through training that will continue over many years you should be able to reach the point where you will be incapable of walking on to the stage with cramped muscles. But you must also have a very strong desire to accomplish this.

You cannot imagine what a joy it is for a person who has used his voice and his body badly all his life, suddenly to feel that he is doing it well. Fortunately it is possible to attain control of one's body and speech, to perfect one's physical apparatus and inner capacities. But to do this requires tremendous discipline and system in your work.

When, however, it is accomplished, you will step on to the stage and will not have to make any effort to act. You will only have to move your eyes, and the eyes of two thousand people in the audience will follow you. You will be pensive—and they will be pensive with you.

To have the right to go on to the stage, not do anything and yet be living in such a way that the entire audience does this in unison with you—that is a great joy! But in order to experience it you must know what your purpose was in going on the stage. The actor who comes on the stage has it in his power to make people think, suffer, be joyful along with him. What is it that confers this power on an actor and gives him the right to carry the spectators with him?

I once wrote about being on my way home one night from an unsuccessful rehearsal in Leningrad, and how I found people sitting around a fire on Michael Place. It was winter and cold. I entered into conversation with them. It transpired that since early evening they had been taking turns to stand in line for tickets to our play. It made me think: "What would make me stay out in the freezing weather all evening in the street? For the sake of what blessings would I do it?" So you see what responsibility lies on us actors with regard to the public that tomorrow will fill the theatre? What gives us the right to come out on the stage?

In four years, when you will have finished your course, I shall ask you to give me an answer to the question: Why did you enter the theatre? We wanted to act, you will reply. That is a natural and comprehensible wish. But is it enough to make a genuine artist out of you? Of course the footlights, the costumes, the audiences, all that is exciting and flattering. But also it spoils you. Constant show of yourselves, compliments—you get so accustomed to them you can scarcely live without them. If after the performance some old professor wanders into your dressing room to tell you that you acted badly in this or that place, and that you need something different for your part—that will be of greater value to you than the screams of your psychopathic admirers who appear to make the reputation of an actor. When Tamagno sang in Moscow, a thunderous voice came from the audience at one of his performances. It was that of an admirer yelling: "Tamagno, bravo! bravo!" I recognized the voice because I had heard it at other performances by other artists. This person ran from theatre to theatre screaming "bravo" and going mad with excitement. There are many like that.

Some actors think that such screaming is an advertisement for them. No. An actor grows as long as he works. If he is going to be greedy for the applause of his admirers his stature will be

lessened. I know one actor who exchanged the society of cultivated and challenging friends for that of ecstatic admirers. As an
actor he became negligible.

Oscar Wilde is quoted as having once said: "An actor is either
a showman or a creator, a priest or a fool." Don't be actors who
are fools. Don't try to cater to the taste of the public, but listen to
the opinion of those who know.

So you will have to decide: Why did I go on the stage? You
may say stupid things. If you do, the others will answer back,
but you must think and talk about this subject constantly. That
"why" will be your main motivation and guide. We shall call it
your super-objective. Keep your mind constantly on the super-
objective of your life.

You have a group newspaper; write in it and decide why you
came into the theatre. Your joint work and the reason for your
going on the stage are your fundamental problems. You must
think, write, talk about them, not only in school but all during
your creative life.

Unless you set these two problems squarely before yourselves
and keep strengthening the super-objective of your life, your first
success will turn your head, and the second will put you off it
entirely. Incidentally a little head-turning does not constitute a
real danger, if you are able to take yourselves in hand in time.

You are lucky. You have a studio into which you can bring
the very best that is in you. When you enter, along with your
rubbers, leave all that is petty and mean outside, bring inside only
your very best feelings and share them with your friends. Here
you will be able to commune with such great geniuses as Shakespeare, Pushkin, Gogol, Ostrovski. In this building you will
become cultivated people, and you will create an atmosphere
which will keep it always clean.

Nevertheless there are always those who enjoy collecting all
sorts of filth and bringing it here to dump within the walls of our
theatre. It will be your job to chase right out of this place the

person who comes to spit, no matter how talented he may be. The talented person who brings filth into our place of work is poisonous because he uses his talent to spread contamination. He may be very much needed here, but he must be gotten rid of without delay. You must not tolerate anyone sitting beside you who will poison the air in our theatre. You must also see to it that if any of you, for any reason, have difficulties at home, you must at least be made to feel at ease here.

Every actor should feel that it is on the stage that art is created; otherwise he is no actor.

Remember always that your strength lies in your unity, and that you came here to perform a great and fine piece of work.

This is my testament to you, wrought out of my experience of fifty-six years of work in this seething caldron which is the theatre.

(1935)

Opera Rules

Concert music is pure music. By contrast opera music is subject to theatrical rules. These rules are to the effect that every scenic performance is action, hence the division into *acts*.

In revivifying opera productions the point of departure should be the music. The objective of the director of an opera is to sift out the *action inherent in the musical picture* and restate this composition of sounds in terms of the dramatic, that is to say the *visual*.

In other words: the action should be determined to a far greater degree by the musical score than merely by the text. The objective of the director is to explain exactly what it is that the composer wished to say when he wrote each phrase of his score, and what dramatic action he had in mind, even though this last may have been only subconsciously in his mind.

The whole point is to convert a concert in costume, which is what most opera performances are nowadays, into a genuine, dramatic spectacle. In this respect I believe that there is no basis for dividing operas into operas for singing and musical dramas, for *every* opera is a musical drama.

The chief exponent of the action in an opera is the *singer-actor,* not the conductor who often misses the point of dramatic action. His role is at present somewhat overestimated. In my opera theatre in Moscow the conductor not only has that title but is also called "Musical Director" of the production because he carries the responsibility for *organizing* the action on the stage to correspond with the intention of the music.

The most necessary item of equipment for an operatic artist is, beyond all doubt, a well-placed voice which enables him to sing both vowels *and consonants*. The consonants are the more important because they are what carry through the volume of the orchestral accompaniment. The famous singer Battistini owed the volume of his voice to his ability to reinforce his tone through consonants. Tamagno, who was no less famous in his day, was able to produce an instantaneous effect with his first words in Verdi's *Otello,* not only because of the perfection with which he sang the beautiful phrase, but also because he pronounced the words *correctly and expressively.*

Tamagno was a dramatic and magnificent Othello in opera because he studied his role with the great tragic actor Salvini, and his musical mentor was Verdi himself. Another master of diction is Chaliapine, who perhaps does not know the exact rules but because he has an intuitive genius he is able to find the right expression and achieves by this means an unparalleled effect.

The production notes of Richard Wagner contain among other things, the secret of producing an opera. You can bring Wagnerian heroes to life and make human beings out of them if you can wean them from everything "operatic" and plan their actions in consonance with the *inner meaning* of the music and not the *external* effects.

I shall attempt to explain this fundamental proposition of how to direct an opera and base one's work on the meaning of the music, by a few examples:

What does one usually see in the scene of the ball in Tschaikowsky's *Eugene Onegin?* Mostly senseless cross movements in which the thread of the action is lost. Yet in reality the ball is merely the *background for the action* which develops in the front of the stage.

One can ask, how do musical themes determine the action?

Actually the very beginning of this act has its *dramatic significance* because the curtain rises with the first notes of the music. Tatiana's love-motif, which you hear in the orchestra, must be expressed on the stage. Tatiana, wrapped in thought, is standing behind one of the columns, looking at Onegin, the object of her girlish love. Then you hear the orchestra play the waltz theme.

Interspersed with snatches of the waltz you hear the agitated strings conveying the turbulent excitement of the young girls who love dancing and military bands. They dance upstage where the ball is beginning.

The serious, long-drawn-out theme in the orchestra is embodied on stage by the slow and dignified crossing of the elderly landowners. A flirtatious music phrase is reproduced by the flirtatious gesture of Olga, who is engaged in a squabble with her fiancé Lenski. This scene, as well as the quarrel between Onegin and Lenski, is played around a large table downstage. In this way the public gets a better understanding of the dramatic idea of the composer.

Take another example: the fourth act of Puccini's *La Bohème*. A quantity of empty bottles and dishes should transport us at once into the centre of bohemian life. The music shows us the excited state of young people which reaches its climax in the dancing scenes. The music thunders and the actors are uproarious. Instead of the usual dances they concoct a so-called "elephant." One actor lies on the ground and puts up his arms and legs, on which a second actor stretches himself while a third turns handsprings. At this moment they carry in the dying Mimi. Death is thus received with an incongruous grimace. Just these contrasts produce the strongest effects.

The so-called "Revenge Duet" in the third act of *Rigoletto* is usually looked upon as a bravura piece for an effective finale. I stage it as the outbreak of resentment of slaves against the tyranny of the duke. Rigoletto is not just one court jester there on the stage; he represents a mass of jesters, of whom there were usually many at such courts, who gnash their teeth and share Rigoletto's emotions in this unheard-of outburst of helpless rage. But Rigoletto remains the *central* figure. The crescendo of the music gives him the opportunity to portray a crescendo of dramatic action.

(1930)

42

The Bond Between Music and Action

In opera I take my point of departure from the music, I try to discover what it was that prompted the composer to write his work. Then I try to reproduce this in the action of the singers. If the orchestra plays a prelude, introducing a scene before the action begins we are not content to have the orchestra simply play this, we put it into scenic terms, in the sense of actions, words, phrases. Thus we often use action to illustrate other instruments which lend color to the orchestra. If an instrument gives the theme of death, the singer will feel the corresponding emotions. He must not disregard these preludes and use the time to clear his throat or prepare his entrance, he must already be part of the unbroken pattern, of the unfolding life of a human spirit in his part, in the play.

The bond with the music must be so close that the action is played in the same rhythm as the music. But this should not be rhythm for the sake of rhythm, as so often is the case. I would like this union of rhythm [of action] and music to be imperceptible to the public. We try to have the words merge with the music and be pronounced musically. There must be an imperceptible coincidence of the movement of rhythm with the music. Nevertheless it must also lend harmony, precision and finish to the singer's acting.

Since I look upon opera as the collective creation of several arts, the words, the text, diction must be as well worked out as possible on the part of the singer. The public must understand everything that is transpiring on the stage. All these objectives of course, represent the ideal towards which we are all striving. Young artists will not achieve perfection immediately, but they must come closer and closer to it all the time. I even wish to have every word of the ensemble and chorus singing made intelligible. This can often be accomplished, but not always. During a *forte* and great *tessitura* one voice caps the other. Time will have to help us solve this difficulty. The dances, as for instance in *Bride of the Tsar* or *Eugene Onegin,* will be performed by the singers themselves.

—Remarks given at the opening of the State
Opera Studio-Theatre (23 November 1926)

Technique of the Creative Mood

Never pretending to be a god or able to hand down gifts from on high, I nevertheless put to myself the following question: Are there no technical means by which the actor can achieve the creative mood, so that inspiration may appear oftener than is its wont? This does not mean that I could create inspiration by artificial means. That would be impossible. What I have wanted to learn was how to create at will a condition favourable to the appearance of inspiration, a condition in the presence of which inspiration was most likely to flow into the actor's soul... and make this no longer a matter of mere accident.

Physical Action as a Means to an End

Remember how an airplane takes off: it has a long runway on which to gain momentum. Currents of air are developed which lift its wings and raise it up off the ground.

An actor too has as you might say his runway, he travels along the line of physical actions to gain momentum. Meantime, with the aid of the circumstances set up by the playwright, magic "ifs," the actor opens out his wings of faith which carry him up into the realm of imagination he so sincerely believes in.

But if the airplane had no solid runway could it get off the ground? Of course not. That is why our first concern is with the building of a solid runway, compounded of physical actions made concrete by their own truthfulness.

Actually there are no physical actions divorced from some desire, some effort in some direction, some objective, without one feeling inwardly a justification for them; there is no imagined situation which does not contain some degree of action of thought: there should be no physical actions created without faith in their reality, consequently a sense of truthfulness. All this bears witness to the close bond between physical action and all the so-called "elements" of the inner creative state.

One of the important elements in the process of achieving an inner creative state is *logic, consistency*. Consistency of what? Of thought, feeling, action (inner and external), desires, objectives, aspirations, imagination, etc., etc.

46

Except in certain instances everything in life has a logical sequence, hence it should also obtain on the stage. Yet how can we instill the sense of the need for this logic and consistency in a student actor?

We do it through the means of physical action. Why physical and not psychological or other inner "elements"?

Have you not noticed that it is more difficult for us to define what we *feel* than what we *do* in exactly the same set of circumstances? Why is this?

Because it is easier to lay hold of physical than psychological action, it is more accessible than elusive inner feelings. Also physical action is easier to fix, it is material, visible. Actually there is no physical action which does not involve desires, aspirations, objectives, or feelings which justify the action; there is no act of imagination which does not contain some imagined action. In the generation of physical actions there must be a faith in their actuality, a sense of truth in them.

All this bears witness to the intimate tie between physical action and all the inner "elements" of a creative state.

We are more at home in the area of physical actions. . . . We can better orient ourselves, we are more inventive, confident, than in the area of the inner "elements" which are so difficult to seize and hold.

It is this accessibility of physical action which prompts us to have recourse to it now in developing in our students a sense of the necessity of logic and consistency.

—from *Othello* production notes (1929-30)

47

Talent, Inspiration and Professionalism

Oh, how seldom does anything happen all by itself in the theatre, or in the role of even the most gifted actor.... It does happen, but not often. To know how to work, really to make an effort—that takes talent too. Even an enormous talent. Inspiration is born of hard work. It is not the other way around.

Professionalism is a very necessary and healthy basis to begin any work, in any field of art....

(Undated)

Back to Work–The Beginning
of the Season

Tomorrow the season begins.

I came back to town today. My nerves are calmed down, as from a night's sleep, they don't react to impressions, it's as if they had lost the habit during the summer. The coming season is exciting although the thought of it is frightening. The future beckons, it promises new impressions, interesting emotions, yet at the same time it frightens you with doubts, disillusion, the wounding of your actor's best and morbidly sensitive feelings.

You feel physical fear too. You fear for your own powers. It seems as if they could not hold up for ten months of heavy work, and besides you must not fall ill during the season. You become over-alarmed, ridiculously cautious over the possibility of catching a cold or getting some infection, and that's depressing.

"If only I can get into harness again," you say, trying to calm yourself as you lie on the sofa in your empty town apartment and listen to the steady racket of noise in the street.

Indeed it is very important for an actor to get back into his work. It costs him a great deal to go out onto the stage after a long period of not having done it, and how easy it is to act a whole play once the season is in full swing. It's a wonderful but also a terrifying feeling to know that the curtain is about to open. Deep down inside you some nerves tremble. You have to steel yourself inwardly so that the trembling will not spread and take control of your whole body.

There is the assistant stage director trying to look not only calm, but lighthearted as he whispers his last directions: the buzz

49

of audience voices, which seems so maliciously cheerful, gradually
dies down with the lowering of the house lights. In this moment
you lose yourself, you turn into some other person, a trusting and
modest person. If the stagehand standing by the curtain ropes
would tell me in this moment that I am a great actor, I would
believe him. Such flattery would bring up my spirits. If he should
tell me I have no gift at all for the stage I would run right away.

Just before the curtain goes up I cannot believe that art can
afford any happy time, and mentally I curse myself for the error of
my ways and I promise myself firmly that never again will I put
myself through such moral torture.

"Going up," whispers the assistant director as he skips off into
the wings, and the tips of the moving curtain seem to flow after
him.

Now you begin to reach around inside your physical self for a
centre in which to gather up and take hold of the reins of your
scattered nerves. When they are put under the control of that
centre your equilibrium and self-mastery are established. For a
second you are embarrassed. You do not recognize your own voice
and intonations, but you soon grow accustomed to it, you begin
to act and you reach a point where you do not even wish to leave
the stage. The trouble is to find your own centre and collect all
your reins: unbridled nerves cannot be directed, they can harass
and throw even the most experienced actor off balance.

At such times anything can go through your mind. You think
you have forgotten your part, your pulse begins to pound in your
ears and you cannot even hear the prompter. Suddenly, like a
knife the thought flashes through your mind that it is really
shameful to be striking attitudes in front of the public for money.
At this your body becomes wooden and a small voice whispers:
"Look out now, or you'll fluff your lines." Frightened you listen
carefully to the lines and because of this you lose your head and
jumble your words until you are sure that your mind is a blank.
Suddenly in your brain a critical remark is heard: "That was an

awkward gesture . . . quite unsuccessful . . . what a stupid intonation . . . too low . . . how insincere!" That queers everything so
you can scarcely summon the strength to decide to cross the whole
width of the stage. Furniture and props draw you like a magnet
and just for spite make you drop something.

This makes me think of an incident: I was taking part in a
reading with a much respected older actor. We both were reading
the verses of a certain famous poet whose memory was being
honoured on this occasion by a select public. There was some kind
of a mixup and we had to wait several hours before appearing.
I was exhausted with waiting and he was wrapped up in telling
me long stories about his difficult, unsettled life. He remembered
some recent bereavement and wept. Just then we were called to
go onto the stage. He became flustered, powdered his eyes and
went on without being able to prepare himself at all.

"Take along the book," I whispered to him just as he went on,
"there isn't any prompter."

"Nonsense . . . I've recited this a couple of hundred times in
public. I learned it by heart when I was a schoolboy." With that
he rejected the book and went on.

He got stuck on the fourth verse, grew pale, paused but went
on. On the tenth verse the same thing happened. He walked in
an unnatural gait, instinctively, over to the prompter's box and
was silent. So was the audience.

After a pause he began the whole poem over again. I tried to
prompt him but he did not hear me. At the tenth verse his voice
wavered and he stopped short in the same place as before.

The audience began to laugh, and after a lengthy pause he
quit the stage. He rushed up to me, snatched the book from my
hand and went back on the stage a second time, walking in a very
defiant way: then he stopped and began to look for his place in
the text. The audience waited patiently as he turned the pages but
he could not find the poem, so he carelessly threw the book at the

nearest chair. It fell to the ground and a laugh broke from the audience.

Pale and almost staggering he now walked to the footlights, almost brazenly struck an attitude with his hand in his vest, in the pose of a third rate raconteur, and rapidly, unintelligibly, began once more to recite the poem from the beginning. At the tenth verse he stopped, the audience then began to prompt him in loud tones clearly mixed with ridicule and malice. He couldn't hear anything. He just stood there. The public roared with laughter. Then he turned and walked to the opposite side of the stage, obviously avoiding any meeting with me. The dreadful part of it was that the door was nailed shut. He tried to open it, tried again, then he froze stock still. The auditorium was absolutely silent.

After a bit he turned and left the stage, a broken, old man. He squeezed through between the curtain ropes and the first wing. Such things are the nightmare fears of an actor.

Dear God! Is art worth all these sacrifices of health, nerves, peace of mind, agonies! My reason says: "No, it is not worth it," but my heart protests that it is.

Again a whole train of thoughts and emotions has been started —how well the actor knows them. But the public does not and I am envious of it although at the same time I pity it. For in these emotions lie the charms and sufferings of the actor.

The theatre!

At that exclamation I turned over on my sofa, stretched myself out with greater ease, and started to talk aloud to myself as though I wanted the people who do not feel the impact of that important word for actors to hear me.

For the public the theatre is a building, a large and well appointed part of which is assigned to its use, while a smaller, not well appointed, rather dirty part serves the purposes of art.

The public is separated from the actors by tightly closed doors bearing the inscription: "Entrance Forbidden to Unauthorized

Persons," also by a curtain which sometimes is raised and sometimes drawn. The public finds it interesting to lift, surreptitiously, a corner of the curtain and glimpse the closed-off, mysterious little world of the actors, where they work while others rest, where it is so brightly lighted during the evenings and so very dark all day, where they say there is so much beauty and darkness, brilliance and dust!

In the theatre the actors put on a show and the audience comes to see it and be entertained by it. Some aver that this pastime is a good thing, that it educates a person. Others assert that the theatre is for amusement, it exists solely for pleasure. Still others derive nothing except boredom out of it at all.

There are various kinds of performances in the theatre. In some they dance, or sing to the accompaniment of an orchestra, sometimes they just chat or do gymnastics, or tricks, sometimes all these things are mixed in together, simultaneously. Each one of these spectacles has its own generally accepted name, and each form of theatre art in turn has its subdivisions according to the sad or comic impression the spectacle is supposed to produce.

Educated people always frequent theatres. They are even inclined in their youth to be very much taken with the theatre, and in some rare instances this love lasts into their middle or even advanced years.

Since ancient times the world geniuses have dedicated their works to the scenic arts, yet the theatre, which reproduced those works in terms of flesh and blood often serves as a haunt for the dregs of society, as a breeding place for the worst of its vices. The art of the stage afforded women the opportunity of independent work and equal terms with men, yet at the same time nowhere are their rights so ruthlessly trampled under foot, or their freedom so curtailed as within the walls of the theatre.

"What then is the theatre and what does it represent?" asks the public in dismay. Should one call it a temple of art or a den of iniquity? Is it a harmful or useful institution? Does it educate or does it pervert? Should we tear down all the buildings of existing theatres or should we put up palaces or temples for it?

The theatre!

For the actors that is quite a different, a really significant word.

The theatre is one large family where you live together in closest harmony or where you engage in mortal quarrels.

The theatre is a beloved woman, sometimes capricious, ill-tempered, ugly and selfish; sometimes fascinating, tender, generous and beautiful.

The theatre is an adored child, unconsciously cruel and artlessly charming. His whims demand everything and you cannot refuse him anything.

The theatre is a second home, it nourishes you and it drains all your forces.

The theatre is a source of heartaches and of immeasurable joys.

The theatre is air and wine, which we must breathe in frequently and be intoxicated by.

Anyone who experiences this deep and rapturous emotion will not escape the theatre, as anyone who is indifferent to it had better avoid this beautiful and cruel art.

My thoughts are interrupted by a loud bell. A letter is brought in to me. I read the following:

Dear Mr. Stanislavski:

I want very much to join your theatre. To be sure I am not deceiving myself, I know that I do not possess any talent, but still I very much want to join it. Even when I was very small I wanted to be an actress, but Mama wouldn't let me and I was sent away to school. Now Mama sees that I am no good at my lessons and has consented to my going on the stage. When I come to your theatre, Mr. Stanislavski, I get the feeling that you could teach me to act. Forgive me for goodness' sake, for bothering you with my request. I'm awfully awfully to blame, but you are a real artist and you will understand."

The first swallow of the season, I say to myself. Poor victim of our cruel but lovely art.

Yet I must confess that this touchingly naïve letter from a girl who has not yet finished school did make an impression of me.

Perhaps this is the first page of the drama of her unfolding life. And besides, who knows . . . perhaps this is a modest call from a genuine talent. . . .

As soon as I sniffed the beginning of the season in the air I was drawn to the theatre, I started out for one of the summer theatres as the winter ones were still closed. A company famous for farce and vaudeville, under the heading of "Satires and Their Morals," was giving some kind of a play translated from the French. At the end of the performance the public was promised a variety show— a "monster gala" "with the participation of . . ." and there followed the list of divas, stars, celebrities and prize-winning beauties. The bottom of the advertisement was decorated with gold letters, bursting bombs, and in inch-high type was printed:

"Unheard of! Unheard of! Fireworks display! Vulcan and the Crater! 50,000 fireworks! 1001 nights! Refreshments will be served by A, wines by B. Private Rooms." . . . Under the Management of so and so, the organizer is such and such, finally the signature of a well known Moscow promoter.

The manager himself greeted me at the box office, and in accordance with theatre custom, offered me a free ticket.

"No, I wish to pay for my ticket, today is a holiday and I imagine you will sell out," I said in refusing his offer.

"You must be our guest! As for the theatre I cannot boast too much. People come, but not enough to crowd the place. The weather is warm, the public prefers to go for a walk, and the company, I may say, has not proved itself . . ." here the management added an unprintable expression.

55

"But the variety show should bring them, that I can boast about!"

With that the management bowed and left, having been called away to deal with a drunk. I went into the theatre.

It would be difficult to relate the contents of the farce, and more so to describe the acting. It is much easier to describe all, or nearly all, performances of this kind.

The leading characters of a farce are: the husband who wants to be a bit of a Don Juan away from his jealous wife. Sometimes the husband is young, usually he is old. If he is young his wife will be of corresponding age. Hers is a benevolent, tearful, dull part. If she is an older woman and ugly the part gains interest. When the husband is old the wife is nearly always both old and very ugly, so that this couple will provide the angle of comedy, if only externally. A nephew, a young and rather colourless role, is also standard equipment. He must have the traditional fiancée, who is charming in her ignorance of the secrets of connubial life and hence, of the point of the play.

They have doctors, friends of the family, in the play just in case . . . so that they can complicate the plot, and principally both to tie knots in it and then untie them. A stupid man or woman servant is essential to the exposition of the plot.

Another necessity in the cast is a rich uncle with the title of Admiral of the Swiss Navy on the Lake of Geneva, or some less involved rank. The centre of the show, around which the whole plot revolves, is a female in good looking clothes, or, if possible, without any. Whoever she may be in the play, a countess or a seamstress, the actress will always play her as a cocotte.

Of course the whole affair cannot be settled without the police.

I shall mention the principal props and effects: men's trousers and women's drawers, forgotten gloves, stockings, garters, a torn skirt, letters lost somewhere on the stage, the sound of a slap administered off stage, visiting cards for the seconds in a duel, a candlestick with a burnt out candle for the husband.

In farces the audiences laugh at the discomfiture, the mis-adventures of the husband who goes off on a spree without the wife's knowledge. The poor fellow is forever being shoved into clothes closets or under the bed, or being carried out in a laundry basket with soiled clothes; people sit on him, splash him with water or slops; they mislay his trousers and he falls into the hands of the police without any on, or he jumps out the window. More than once a harassed husband has brought down the curtain on a farce by promising never again to break his marriage vows, but —alas!—this promise lasts only to the next play where the whole story is told over again in a different setting.

A talented actor is expected to be able to say silly things with a serious face, and tell spicy stories with a naïve expression, to make unnatural things seem natural, make something dull appear to be gay, give the aspect of wit to banalities—in a word he is supposed to edit the author or, better still, replace him. Then the purpose is achieved, the play draws crowds, and the audience laughs a lot during the first act, less in the second and not at all in the third.

After a very long intermission the "divertissement" began.

The scene represented a fantastic garden. The wings were made of roses and about fifteen feet high. The flowers ranged from white through all sorts of shades up to and including gold. There was a fountain made of tinfoil and silver threads in the centre, and behind were ranged a lot of little gold sofas and chairs. The backdrop represented some kind of terrace and weird architecture, also a red curtain with gold tassels was painted on it. The artist had kindly raised one side of it and through the perspective thus afforded one could glimpse in the distance mountains, rivers, ripening grain, lakes, roads, valleys, forests, plowed fields, birds in flight, the sky, clouds; in the far distance the Kremlin of Mos-cow, and perhaps even the Eiffel Tower. In the midst of this marvelous garden hung a trapeze, decorated with roses, and the general beauty of the scene was enhanced by some loud music: a march or a polka, with castanets.

Out came an athletically built, elderly man with a battered face, in a dark blue suit that looked like a footman's livery, with silver buttons. He had many medals on his chest. He was followed by a woman who skipped in after him with a masculine caper. She had been beautiful, she had a powerful build and heavy legs. She forced a smile. She was leading a wiry, skinny, unhealthy looking little girl, whose tired face was coarsely rouged. Both mother and daughter were dressed in grass-coloured tights covered with spangles. The husband politely helped his wife up on to the rope, and she despite her years lightly pulled herself up by her hands to the ceiling and settled herself on the trapeze. Because the child was so little and weak in build they hauled her up.

It was really amazing to see the adroitness with which that mother constantly watched over the little girl, saving her from falling and certain death. The excited audience, along with the child, lived through dangerous moments and applauded them both. Thank goodness it all ended well and the mother and father with the child on his shoulders bowed themselves out, much applauded by the audience.

It does happen—fortunately it is a very rare occurrence—that a child is not caught in time, falls, and is either killed outright or crippled for life before the very eyes of a horrified audience. Then they whistle and show their indignation, but it is too late. Of course the mother can fall too or they can fall together. Usually it is the dignified father who falls, but he does it to get a laugh; after all he has to earn his daily bread.

Then the trapeze was flown, the father dragged the rope off with him, and the first number on the programme was over.

The orchestra played a very gay tune. From the wings emerged an exquisite Frenchwoman who immediately bowed to everyone as if they were all her very good friends. By the time she reached the second verse of her song the public was enchanted by her pertness, by the third they were roaring with laughter, by the fourth they had whipped out their opera glasses and were enjoying the details of this spicy morsel. She, meanwhile, was making roguish eyes and had had time to lift a corner of her short gauzy skirt and reveal a beautiful leg in gossamer stockings and some kind of very special panties. She did all this very simply, artlessly and charmingly and the public was convinced it was quite all right for a woman to come out on the stage and show off her panties.

This number was called: "New! New! New! A Parisian Diva, Mademoiselle———, known as the Girl Wonder. The Diamond Queen in her repertoire!"

Judging by the program which was studded with advertisements, the next artist was supposed to be a celebrity, because her name, which was printed in heavy type, was flanked with two red hands and pointing fingers.

Out came a gawky, thin woman. The orchestra struck up some plaintive music: it was the song of the beggar boy. He and his aged grandmother are dying of hunger. He is sent out to beg. Weak, shivering, he stands in the cold rain and whispers with a trembling voice: "Help me for Christ's sake!" Grudgingly a small coin is given to the poor boy, he coughs and can scarcely get the words out: "Help me for Christ's sake!"

The boy steals to feed his dying grandmother. He is caught and taken to the police station. There the sergeant cross-questions him. Tears and coughing make it impossible for him to reply, but the singer's eyes, full of tears, plead for him: "Forgive him for Christ's sake! Forgive him for Christ's sake!"

The boy dies in prison and appears before the Judgment Seat— he is frightened, upset, trembling. His lips scarcely move, but probably he is trying to say: "Forgive me for Christ's sake!"

A beautiful deep voice tells him he is forgiven and has expiated all his sins through his sufferings on earth. A few tears trickled down my own cheeks and for a long time in my ears I heard that pitiful, weak voice: "Forgive me for Christ's sake! Forgive me for Christ's sake!"

After that they showed a talking walrus.

I left the theatre with a headache just when a cannonade was going off: "Fireworks!" "Vulcan and the Crater!" Explosions, hissing sounds, the swish of rockets, the rasping of pinwheels— they all went straight to the painful spot in my head and acted on my nerves, painfully frayed by the noises of city life. When you hear shots behind you, you involuntarily quicken your steps in the hope that the pinwheel won't fly off and hit you in the back. And so I hurried home. . . .

It was two when I put out my light, but I could not go to sleep. Little feminine feet, a walrus, men's trousers, "Help me for Christ's sake," the monster-gala, the letter from that schoolgirl, the problems of art, "et v'la comment on finit l'Cancan" . . . the pinwheel, theatre season . . . a blow—and I jumped up and stared into the dark.

It ended by my sitting on the edge of my bed and smoking in the dark while I did some thinking.

Good God! What is the theatre coming to! Is it worth all the sacrifices which we place on its altar?

In his working hours, which means all through the season, an actor is not a normal person. It is just as though another person has entered his being and taken over its control. His body wants to lead its usual life and moves by habit, but the new master isn't concerned with that, he goes about his own affairs. He brazenly occupies all the interstices of the brain, searching about in them for lost memories. Joy alternates with despair as familiar images of bygone experiences loom in his memory and then are wrapped again in mist. . . . He answers questions mechanically, but without making any sense. He takes a cab without telling the driver where to go . . . and life seems to break off somehow. . . .

There is somebody bowing to him . . . he raises his own hand mechanically . . . but why . . . why do it. . . . He raises his hat and crosses himself. . . . No, that was not what he meant to do! . . . He makes a gesture dismissing the whole thing. . . . What is he doing! . . . They'll take me for a madman! He comes to for a moment and realizes what is going on. . . . "Yes, yes, someone went by and I did not raise my hat but crossed myself instead. How silly!" He thinks his friend will be angry and think he is either too proud or too drunk to bow. He thinks he was probably playing a little scene in his cab, making all sorts of grimaces. . . . And everyone saw him. . . . How embarrassing! "How do you do." He raises his hat. . . . Who was it went by? The face was familiar. Ah yes! It was the man who sat in the second row from the side at those first performances. He used to clap so hard one wished almost that he wouldn't. . . . An unpleasant personality! How astonished he must have been at my bowing to him—What am I saying! That's the man who lives in the country and whom I met in the train . . . he was taking home a toy sickle! But I don't know him. Ah, that's a good make-up. . . . The face is young, the eyes are old, they have seen a lot. . . . That's good . . . that will come in handy. . . . Now if he were in love and looked at her with those eyes . . . he would be repulsive. That's just right for a part. . . .

"Hey, stop! Where are you taking me? Where did I tell you to go? To the theatre? And where are we? These are the outskirts of the city!"

"You didn't tell me anything."

"You are absolutely stupid." You try to reason with the driver but you are not sure to whom your remark applies.

"Well, what am I to do?"

"Turn around. . . . Wait a moment, where are we? You'll make me late. . . . I did not have a moment to spare. . . ."

Lateness for one appointment pushes another out of place or overlaps it. . . . You feel you have detained everyone, you can see by their faces that they are tired of waiting; you hurry, you get flustered . . . you finish one meeting but forget to say the most important thing; you get names mixed up . . . and that produces fresh complications. . . .

This irresponsible state goes on until that intruder inside you ceases his unmannerly and constant work.

A new period commences. To what can this state be compared?

Imagine that you are looking for a melody you once heard. It teases you all day, but you cannot quite get it back. You stumble across some memory or other, perhaps the corner of a room with a plush sofa. What's the relation of that? Or the dark-blue glasses of a certain man. Ah yes, was he the one? . . . At that instant you get hold of a melody. Now you remember it was an evening gathering and someone sang. But what has the carved what-not to do with it? And again you recall the musical transition and it keeps running in your head for a long time. It's true it was in the daytime; I can see a ray of sunshine flooding a room. . . . It is only towards evening and without any reason at all that you find what you are looking for. It is a certain aria which was played on a gramophone in a neighbouring house, and the gentleman with the dark glasses rode in the streetcar with you, and you looked at his dark glasses while inside you were busily hunting for your melody. Now you know it from beginning to end you can even picture to yourself the notes on the score, just as you would if you were going to publish the aria. You sing it and sing it. . . . As you go to bed you sing, when you get up you sing. . . . You cannot stand it any more, you are bored to death with the aria, and yet you go on singing it. . . . Tara . . . ta . . . ta . . . ti . . . ti . . . tu . . . Tu-tu-ruti-tata.

In this new period of creative work there will be a moment just like the finding of the melody. How wonderful it is to grow up all at once and understand everything down to the last details! What people really are, how they feel, their habits, their surroundings, the way the whole house is built, etc., etc. In this blessed period everything smiles at you, you even laugh at the very thought of how much it is like what your imagination discovers.

But then comes the third period. Here you hasten to write down everything you have seen or felt. No time must elapse or you will lose what you have found, the charm of the vividness of your impressions. You write for days on end, never mind the grammar or the phrasing. And what a style it is! For instance: "He stood with his head bent over his knee," I wrote once, "and she the opposite." This was perfectly clear to me and still is, but only to me.

Then comes the time of putting it all into physical terms. A most harrowing time for the director of the play. It is hard to convey to anyone else one's feelings in all the scarcely perceptible details.

To what can this new state be compared?

Imagine that you must save a friend and that his fate lies in the hands of a third person. This last, however, is a foreigner; he is a man of entirely different character from you or your friend, he has other views on life and quite other convictions. On top of all that he is scarcely acquainted with your mother tongue and you are not familiar at all with his language. The circumstances of the case are complicated and thorny. An explanation is initiated. With every phrase you run into unfamiliar words, and in order to replace them you resort to every possible means of communication and even use facial expressions and gestures. After a prolonged effort you succeed in explaining some of your message, but the most delicate and ticklish part you still cannot transmit and you are forced to be content with patching up some degree of harmony between your friend and the foreigner.

By friend I mean the author of the play. And the foreigner is the actor on whom the fate of the whole play depends. The position of the director of the play is made still more difficult by the fact that he is not dealing with just one person but a whole company of actors, with scene designers, property men and other

63

participants in the enterprise. To each and every one of them he must outline his production plan in all its intangible details and help to put it in substantial form. Echoes from the nervous strain the director and the actors are under are relayed to their families. I can only be grateful for the patience shown by mine.

In order to understand what a director or an actor goes through when he is not understood, watch him during the dress rehearsals and the first performance. I really think that the commander of a regiment, watching a battle in progress, does not go through a greater ordeal. I believe that a mother who is present at an operation on her son suffers the same way. There is not a look of anguish that does not distort the director's face when he sees how his creation, his friend, is being mangled. He sits in a cramped position, clutching the arm of his seat, his arms and legs twitching, the way you watch some great weight when it threatens to crush someone; you make the same movements, unconsciously trying to ward off the danger.

"Good work, good work!" the director whispers to himself with a sigh of relief. "Thank you, thank you, that was fine, darling. . . . Oh, he's killed it! The wretch!" and with another spasm his whole body falls back in the chair and beads of perspiration stand out on his forehead.

In this state he sometimes has to rush out on to the stage to continue in the part he is playing, often the leading part. And even then, at the very moment of making his entrance in the dark of the wings the director does not make way for the actor, on the contrary he interferes with him, because of his habit of watching everything that is going on in every part of the stage. A role which demands the whole being of the actor will not tolerate this double identity and takes its revenge. The director cancels out the actor, the latter must wait his turn. This does not come until about the tenth performance, that is when his function as a director of the play has come to an end. It is only then that the actor in him can work without interference. But this is too late for him to rehabilitate himself in the eyes of the audience. It has already passed judgment on his performance.

"As for Mr. X," you read in the paper, "he was not satisfactory. His performance was pale and vague. Obviously this nice actor does not have the qualities for this type of part." And the majority repeat the sentence.

After this unnatural tension a reaction sets in. The most acute phases of it are manifest in the actor's home life. His family has to deal with a man who is physically exhausted and whose best feelings have been wounded. This gloomy and suffering creature will not open his mouth for days on end, and there is no way of knowing what sad thoughts are passing through his head. Sympathy is out of place—on the contrary it irritates him because it may pick out to praise the very things which run counter to his intentions as a director and they were not understood by the majority. To be sure the play is meeting with success, but the most interesting parts which the director planned for the over-all picture in his production have been lost, and it is as hard for him to become reconciled to this as it is for a mother when she sees her child's arm amputated in order to save his life.

The reaction ends up with a feeling of hatred for the theatre and temporary disillusionment with art.

This is not a happy time for his family as his whole household often gets the brunt of his mood. Having broken with art, he returns to the bosom of his family, and like a naughty schoolboy he hurries to expunge from his record the black mark against his record which he has received in school. The household, in his eyes, is not well run. His great energy is now thrown into putting everything right. His work hums and soon he proudly feels that a home needs the master's attention. Usually, after some major row about household matters, he is told: "You had better stick to your own affairs and let us attend to ours."

It was getting light. My head nestled in the pillow. My dream took full possession of me and all the objects in the room, the walls seemed far away and became transparent. As I drifted farther and farther away from them, I felt myself grow smaller, lighter and freer. . . .

I was wakened early and handed two letters. My head was heavy, it took me quite a while to gather the energy to lift it off the pillow. My dream made me feel tired instead of refreshing me.

During the season this is the usual way you feel in the morning. You feel you will never get through all that is scheduled for the day. But the morning rehearsal pulls your distended nerves together, by evening they are taut, and after the performance they are overstrained. Thus you are always living on nerves borrowed from the next day.

I opened the letters. The first one contained the following:

Dear Mr. Stanislavski:

I have decided to go on the stage so I am enlisting your aid. I am an engineer by profession, and I finished my course because I was told this was absolutely necessary. From that moment I have been in a state of torment. While I was studying I had a goal to reach, now it is gone because I do not like my profession and do not want to continue in it. I have tried out all sorts of other work, carefully omitting acting because I have been told I have no talent. I have been a teacher, a tutor, a salesman, a clerk in various enterprises, but all the time my heart was in the theatre. You need people with an education there and I offer my services. I am not aiming high: ten small roles a year in good productions, and I would be inwardly satisfied. The more work I have to do, the better. On the material side I can do with very little, whatever an unspoiled person of education and training can live on.

In case you are willing to help me with your counsel, kindly reply to the following address..."

In the other envelope I find a note scribbled in pencil on a scrap of none too clean paper, and a picture post card with my likeness: "Sign and return. The address is such and such. —L. M."

I found this curt attitude towards an actor somewhat offensive, and I was on the point of tearing up the envelope, the note and the picture, but then... I remembered the words of a very intelligent woman. She said to me: "Actors who disdain the manifestations of enthusiasm on the part of their public are both wrong and illogical. Either this is affectation on their part or they do not understand their calling. There is no point in creating something with one hand only to destroy with the other all you have built up. Why does an actor try to create an illusion behind the footlights and then destroy it in his ordinary life? If this is done out of vanity, just to play with his disdain of fame—that is very shallow. If it is done out of fastidious distaste for the more vulgar expressions of admiration—then that is unworthy of an actor who should have enough tact and knowledge of people to be able to influence them in the necessary direction. When actors plead lack of time or laziness I do not believe them, if only because these same actors always find time to court their audience when they seek success with it. In the majority of cases the trouble is that actors do not realize the public nature of their mission. This is not ended when they leave the footlights, it is far more widespread, and we know of examples when actors have made use of their charm and popularity to play a part in public life, and so," she said in conclusion, "an actor is obligated to deal warmly with the feelings he has aroused in his admirers, and he should use every opportunity to raise those feelings to an ever higher level."

I put my autograph on the post card and addressed it ready

for mailing, then hurried to dress myself as some ladies were waiting to see me on some business or other.

And who were they? It turned out that one of them was the schoolgirl who sent me that letter yesterday. To bolster her self-confidence she had brought two friends along.

"And so," I began after the usual exchange of courtesies, "you wish to become an actress?"

"Oh yes, yes, I do want to most awfully!" she agreed, and pressed the palms of her hands to her flaming cheeks.

"But you do not want to continue in school?"

She turned to her friend with a kind of childish triumph, as if to say:

"Olga darling! How funny! Everyone pays money to look at actors and here we are . . . actually talking to one!"

"Confess," I continued, "that someone told you that an actress doesn't need any education? And that a genuine talent succeeds by intuition in grasping what others have to learn by hard work and knowledge? They say that such lucky people exist, but alas, they are rare, very rare, and I have never seen a single one."

"No, honestly, no one did," she murmured, "but you talk . . . as if I were . . . somebody special. But really, truly . . . I am awfully, awfully . . . modest."

"Well, don't take on, just calm down."

"Honestly . . . I just decided . . . if I haven't any talent . . . I'll do just mob scenes . . . or the tiniest, most insignificant parts—just weenie ones . . . honestly . . . and yet I'll be so happy, so happy, really awfully so."

"But even such parts call for talent."

"There too?" And the poor thing heaved a heavy sigh.

"What's to be done about it, there's no getting along without talent. Think about it yourself: art is creativeness, and creativeness (be it small or great) is available only to talent, therefore without talent there is no creativeness, and without creativeness no art."

"And what is talent?"

"Talent is the happy combination of many creative capacities in a person, and united with a creative will."

"Will?"

"Of course. You cannot create without the will to do so. An artist must have the desire to create, or be able to arouse this will in himself."

The girl sighed and looked sad. Probably she was bored. She was almost reluctant to ask the next question about an actor's creative capacities.

"There are many of them: notably, the capacity to receive, impress, restudy, analyze, execute, affect the audience."

"I don't understand."

"To put it in other words, an actor has to have: powers of observation, sensitiveness, memory (affective memory), temperament, fantasy, imagination, inner and outer effectiveness, ability to metamorphose himself, taste, intelligence, a sense of inner and outer rhythm and tempo, be musical, sincere, forthright, possess self-control, be inventive, have stage presence, and so on and so forth."

"I really am not very bright," the poor girl admitted, and nearly drilled a hole in her glove with her nail.

"Then you need an education all the more."

"What else?"

"You need expressive qualities to personify the playwright's talented creation, that is to say you must have a good voice, expressive eyes, face, facial expression, body line, plasticity, etc., etc."

"Oh, what a list of things!" she waved her arms in despair.

"Don't be alarmed. . . . Many things are acquired in time and with hard work."

"Besides, you must work all your life to develop your mind and perfect your inner self. You must never despair or give up, and above all you must love your art with all your strength and love it unselfishly."

"Oh, that's not much: I am not worried about that!...I love it, I love it...really awfully!" She cheered up at once and seemed as buoyant as if all obstacles had been cleared away. After thinking for a moment she fell sad again and almost tearfully whispered:

"Well, all right. I'll go on studying....Honestly I will. But... not in school. I'll read and read....I'll read every single play."

"That is not enough. To develop properly you must have general knowledge and study systematically. Whether you receive this education in school or at home makes no difference, the point is that your attitude towards this question must be that of awareness."

"That's fine!" she snatched at my words. "I'll study at home, won't I, Olga? Perhaps with Maria Yegorovna? All right?" And she was as gay as if she had just passed all her examinations.

"But what about talent?" This disturbed her.

"Shall I read something for you? I brought along...but I am so embarrassed, really...it's just awful!..."

I quickly closed the book she had opened and began to explain the conditions of entrance to the school of the Art Theatre and its curriculum of work.

While I was talking the girl, out of boredom, carefully drew a sort of pattern on the cover of her book and became really absorbed in what she was doing. Arkadi!!! Arkasha!!! Arkashonchik!!! was the boy's name I read intertwined with the whole gay pattern she was drawing. I stopped short and stood up, ready to say goodbye.

"But cannot I become an actress?" asked one of the schoolgirl's companions. She was young, not pretty, with red spots instead of pink cheeks on her oldish face.

"They say I have talent," she added, looking at me rather fiercely through her glasses.

The first girl, almost as if on order, rushed at me:

"Honestly, really and truly she has! Varya acted at the Levshins, and did it so well—it was terrible! I even cried. You wouldn't believe it!!"

"You were just wonderful, Varya," echoed the third and rather fat girl, who up to this point had not uttered a word.

We sat down again and the conversation was resumed. Still I did not quite dare say openly:

"Young lady, you would have to possess a very great talent to win over a public with that exterior of yours, with your rasping voice and provincial accent."

But as the talk went on I was obliged at last to hint as much.

"But is actress X beautiful? And yet you accepted her! How silly that I should be upset."

I waited in order to give her time to get out her handkerchief and wipe her tears. She did all this very nervously.

"What part did you play?" I asked almost guiltily, in order to turn the conversation into another channel.

"Catherine, in *The Storm*."

There was a pause.

"How old are you?" said I, feeling more guilty than ever.

"I'll soon be nineteen."

Another awkward pause.

"She was frightfully, frightfully good! I really didn't recognize her. She looks so very tall on the stage. It was really almost scary, wasn't it, Nyuta?"

"Why are you insisting?" I said. "She was good, that's enough."

The fat girl spoke up from the dark recess of a far corner.

"And you, are you thinking of going on the stage?" I asked turning to her.

"No, I am going to college."

"But I won't," Varya burst in. "I just cannot be a trained nurse! I don't care, I just can't!"

I felt a shiver run through me when I heard the emotional outburst. I could see her on the stage—a powerful, unpleasant, neurotic figure.

71

There came into my mind a picture of life in the remote provinces; a nondescript public, scanty art, and in that setting I could hear the sharp hysterical cries of a pale, sickly woman. In a year's time she will have aged, and then she will probably turn up at our theatre. At first she will ask, and later she will beg us, with tears in her eyes, to take her on even with a minimum salary, and not for her sake but for that of her child.

Poor thing! Even then she will find no place on the stage.

"My dear young lady, save yourself. Go to college; you will not find your happiness on the stage," I murmured almost in a whisper, and we parted.

(1907-1908)

Back to Study–Talks with Established Actors

...If all that interests you is the possibility of playing a new role with a slightly refurbished technique then I must disillusion you in advance. I am not getting ready merely to put on another production; such laurels are of no interest to me. Whether I put on one play more or less is of no significance. What I do consider important is that I convey to you all I have accomplished in my lifetime. I want to teach you how to play many parts, not one part. So I want you to think this over. An actor must forever be preparing himself for a higher degree of excellence. He must be always struggling toward achieving, as soon as he can, a mastery over all roles, not just the present one he is to study.

So I beg of you to answer me honestly: do you want to study? All I ask is that you please be frank with me. There is nothing dishonourable in this: you are grown men and women, each of you has a reputation in the profession of acting, each of you has the right to consider himself an accomplished master of his art, and may continue in that mastery to the end of his days. You may be far more attracted to the idea of playing two or three parts brilliantly than undertaking any long-drawn-out and difficult course of study. I understand this point of view perfectly. Have the courage to speak your minds. I should have greater respect for an honest confession than for an insincere compliance with me. ...But at the same time I must in all honesty warn you that unless you do study you will come to a dead end in your creativeness.

The art of the (Moscow) Art Theatre is such that it requires constant renewal, constant persistent work on itself. It is built on reproducing and conveying true organic life. It cannot tolerate the stagnation of traditions even in beautiful forms. It is alive; like all living things, it is forever unfolding, in movement. What was good yesterday is no longer valid today. Today's performance is not what yesterday's performance was. For this type of art a special technique is necessary—not the study of fixed theatrical forms, but a technique of mastery over the laws of the creative nature of man, a capacity to affect that nature, to govern it, the ability to develop one's intuitiveness, one's creative possibilities, in every performance. This is an artistic technique. The qualities which are generated by it should form the basis of the art of our theatre and distinguish it from other theatres. This is fine art. But, and I repeat, it calls for the persistent hard work of an actor on himself, otherwise he very quickly, much more quickly than you imagine, degenerates, becomes a nonentity, and our theatre would fall beneath the level even of the ordinary cliché theatre. It is bound to fall lower because in that theatre there are rigidly fixed craft forms, carefully acquired, hardy traditions, which are transmitted from generation to generation. All that is sufficient to maintain a certain quality, a certain level on which the theatre can continue to exist. Our art is very fragile and if those who create it do not nurture it with constant care, keep it always moving ahead, developing it, perfecting it, it will soon die.

Proficiency in this technique of ours is the job of the entire company, directors as well as actors. Our art is a joint enterprise. It is not sufficient for us to have brilliant individual performances in production. We must conceive of it as a harmonious composition of all elements, a whole artistic achievement.

As I depart this life I wish to turn over to you the bases of this technique. It cannot be transmitted orally, nor in written form of exposition. It must be studied in the work of practical execution. If we achieve good results and you master this technique then you will be able to spread it and inevitably develop it further.

I will give you one "steer": Actually this so-called method sets forth between five and ten commandments to ensure for you the proper approach to all roles during all your lives.

But remember this: every great and meticulous actor should at certain intervals (of perhaps every four or five years) return to his studies. His voice needs to be placed again—it wears out with work. He needs to clear out his creative being from accumulated dross such as vanity, self-adulation, etc., and he must constantly, day by day, increase his cultural value as an artist; that is why an actor should take six months or more off every five years or so and go back to school.

Now do you understand clearly the objective I am setting before you? Let me repeat: do not be thinking in terms of a particular performance; think only of study and more study. If you agree to study let us begin. If not, then let us part in friendly fashion. You will go back to the theatre to continue what you were doing, and I shall gather together some other group and do what I feel is my duty towards art.

(1937)

The Life of a True Artist

...Is it not quite clear now, when you realize all that is required of a true artist, that he must lead a life full of interest, beauty, variety, excitement and enlightenment? He must be aware of what is going on not only in the large cities, but also in all outlying parts of the country, in villages, factories, plants and in the great world centres of culture. Let the actor observe and study the life and psychology of both his own nation and that of foreign nations.... What we (actors) need is a limitless horizon....

...An actor cannot be merely someone, somewhere, at some time or other. He must be I, here, today.

—from conversations with senior actors of the Art Theatre (April 1936)

PART TWO

"The value of any art is determined
by its spiritual content...."

After Ten Years in the Art Theatre

... At this critical point destiny sent us two saviours: Anton Chekhov and S. T. Morozov.

The Seagull flew in from Yalta. It brought us good luck and, like the Star of Bethlehem, lighted the new road we were to travel in pursuit of our art.

Savva Morozov not only came to our support with material help, he also warmed us with his responsive heart and cheered us with the energy of his joyous nature.

(1908)

On the Death of Tolstoy

...I must begin with what is uppermost in my mind. We are alone here, and in sore distress over the news about Tolstoy, which we heard after a delay of two days.

I had not thought it would be so hard to bear.... Only today we learned of what has been going on, where and how the great event took place. I am quite overwhelmed by the greatness and spiritual grandeur of Tolstoy and his death: the clergy, like a thief in the night trying to intrude on the dying man, his pathetic, all too earth-bound family, not daring to enter the now historic house; the regiments of newspaper men, photographers, the curious crowds, wandering around in the dark, whispering while the naïve sage lay there, believing he was quite alone, and was so surprised by the arrival of his son Sergius that he said: "How did you find me?" Then the Government people, the police, leaning over backwards with affability, the attitude of the peasants, the chanting, the absence of the clergy: all this is so extraordinary, so noteworthy, so symbolical, that I can think of nothing else except the great Leo, who died like a King, brushing aside at the end all that was trivial, superfluous, offensive to death. What good fortune to have lived in Tolstoy's day and how terrifying it is to remain on earth without him, as terrifying as to lose one's own conscience and ideals!

Peace be to the dust of this greatest of human beings!

—from a letter to Nemirovich-Danchenko (10 November 1910)

Chekhov's Influence on the Art Theatre

The production of *The Seagull* marked the beginning of the second stage of our artistic development. By this time the management had acquired a certain degree of experience and knowledge.

The actors had learned to handle the basic requirements of the stage. Their temperaments and voices were reinforced, they exercised the necessary self-control, and had learned to metamorphose themselves into stage images; perhaps these were not always profoundly or subtly conceived as to inner content, but they gave proof of vivid imagination and external delineation. All this enabled us to offer them ever more exacting and complex challenges.

The directors of the plays meanwhile had won a certain degree of authority over the company, and that gave them the possibility of beginning to carry through the artistic objectives laid out by the theatre. Moreover they had learned by this time what the stage was capable of presenting from the point of view of living truth.

All this preliminary work fused successfully with the new requirements which Chekhov exacted from our actors.

Chekhov's objectives coincided in turn with those of Shchepkin and hence with those of our own theatre. Consequently Chekhov, Shchepkin, and our theatre were amalgamated into a common effort to achieve artistic simplicity and truthfulness on the stage.

In banishing the old concept of "theatre" from our own theatre Chekhov did not reckon with its rooted conventions. He merely preferred to have fewer of them. He painted pictures from life, not plays for the stage. Therefore he often expressed his thought not in speeches but in pauses or between the lines or in replies consisting of a single word. Since he believed so thoroughly in the power of the theatre's art, and since he was incapable of disjoining man from Nature, from the world of sounds and the things that surround him, he put his confidence not only in our actors but in all those who contribute collectively to our art.

Chekhov was not only a poet in the theatre, he was also a sensitive director, critic, designer and musician. There is a real basis, when one is speaking of Chekhov, for being reminded of a landscape by Levitan and melodies of Tschaikowsky.

All these peculiarities of Chekhov's genius render old methods of interpretation and settings impossible, no matter how excellent they may be in their own way. Gone is the "resounding intonation," the stately tread of actors, their artificial inspiration, the red velvet curtain, the conventional reading of parts in front of the prompter's booth, the elaborate wings and doorways, the theatrical storm and rain—none of that goes with Chekhov's dramas.

Chekhov's characters cannot be "shown," they can only be *lived*. The actor who wants merely to read a part will find no material in Chekhov. Chekhov requires actors who will work with him and complement him.

Consequently at the very moment when *The Seagull* winged its way into our theatre we were in some measure, at least externally, prepared to accept the challenge of Chekhov's dramas.

He succeeded sometimes in turning a stage set into a living landscape, and the theatrical flats into a room. A lifelike setting in turn required a lifelike production and lifelike methods of acting.

The *external* aspects of these demands resulted in making actors turn their backs to the public, walk away from the glaring footlights into the shadows of upstage, play offstage, blend with background and noises—in a word this all gave rise to methods of interpretation quite unknown before Chekhov. These methods are easily acquired by anyone who does not set store by theatrical conventions, who as much as possible even avoids them, who shares Chekhov's own opinion that the less there are of them in the theatre, the better.

The *inner* problems of a Chekhov drama are far more complex. They are of the following nature: To hold a spectator without an interesting plot, without acting for effect, one must attract him through the spiritual and literary quality of the play.

Yet how is that possible? Chekhov's plays are profound in their amorphousness, the characters often feel and think things not expressed in the lines they speak.

Yet to indulge in too hair-splitting analysis, to lay the soul of a character too bare would be to rob Chekhov of his individual, poetically veiled quality. On the other hand nebulousness in his psychology robs an actor of ultimate support in living his part.

What is to be done?

In order to play Chekhov one should inhale the aroma of his emotions, his intimations, interpret the hints of profound but not entirely explicit thoughts. One of the most important means an actor has in experiencing the creation of a Chekhov character is a subtle sensitiveness to the literary quality of the play. In his works Chekhov makes extraordinary and most significant demands of an actor from this literary angle.

To bring a company to this achievement it is not enough to be a teacher and a director, one must also be a man of letters. This distinction in our theatre belongs to Vladimir Ivanovich Nemirovich-Danchenko, to whom also belongs the very idea of the production of *The Seagull*.

Such a combination of demands made on our company—by poets, writers, directors, painters—resulted in the creation of a completely new atmosphere on our stage. Thanks to innumerable experiments, the talent of our actors, their capacity for work and their devotion to the theatre, we succeeded in finding entirely new methods of dramatic interpretation based on the familiar testament of Shchepkin and the innovations of Chekhov.... And these new methods served as the basis for our further artistic progress.

(1908)

83

Memories of Chekhov

When and where did I meet Anton Chekhov? I do not recall. Probably it was in 1889. During the first period of our acquaintance, before the Art Theatre had come into existence, we met occasionally at official dinners, celebrations, in theatres. These meetings left no traces in my memory except in three instances.

I remember meeting Chekhov in the A. S. Suvorin bookshop in Moscow. The owner, at that time also the publisher of Chekhov, was standing in the middle of the room and was berating someone. An unknown gentleman in a black top hat and grey macintosh was standing beside him in a most obsequious pose, holding in his hand a package of books just purchased. And Chekhov was leaning over a counter, examining some bindings and occasionally interrupting A. S. Suvorin with brief phrases which were received with loud guffaws.

The man in the mackintosh was very funny. He rocked so with laughter that he kept dropping his package of books on the counter, and then picking them up when he grew serious again.

Chekhov turned to me too with some kind of jocose greeting but I did not appreciate his humour in those days.

I hate to confess it but at that time I was not drawn to him. He seemed to me proud, haughty and not quite without guile. Perhaps this was due to his trick of throwing back his head— actually the reason why he did it was that he was short-sighted and this enabled him to see better through his pince-nez. Also his habit of looking over the head of the person talking to him or constantly fingering his pince-nez made him seem to me supercilious and insincere, whereas actually this was the result of a really sweet shyness which at the time I did not suspect.

Another meeting of little significance which stuck in my memory, took place in Moscow at the Korsh Theatre in the course of a musical and literary evening for the benefit of a writers' fund (sixtieth anniversary of the death of Pushkin, Jan. 4, 1897). [Stanislavski recited Lermontov's *Death of a Poet*. Ed.] I was appearing for the first time before a real public in a real theatre and I was very much taken up with myself.

On purpose I had not left my overcoat backstage as actors are supposed to do but in the cloakroom of the lobby. I counted on putting it on amid the curious glances of the public I expected to astonish.

Actually it did not turn out that way. I had to hurry away in the hope of being unnoticed. At this critical moment I ran into Chekhov. He came straight to me and greeted me with: "They tell me you play my *Bear* wonderfully. Listen, do play it. I'll come to see it and then I'll write a review of it." He was silent for a moment, then added: "And I'll collect royalties on it." Again an instant of silence, then he concluded: "One ruble and twenty-five kopeks."

I confess that I was hurt because he had not praised the performance I had just finished. Now I remember his words with tender emotions. Probably Chekhov was actually trying to buck me up with his little joke after the failure I had just sustained.

The setting for the third and last remaining meeting which I can recall out of this early period of my acquaintance with Chekhov was the small, cramped office of the editor of a famous review. There were a number of people there I did not know. The place was full of smoke. A well-known architect of the day, a friend of Anton Chekhov, was exhibiting plans for a People's Building, to include a tea room and theatre. I rather timidly crossed swords with him on my special subject.

Everyone listened intently, while Chekhov wandered up and down the room making everyone laugh and, to be quite frank, interfering with everyone. He seemed especially gay that evening:

tall, chubby, red-faced and smiling. At the time I did not grasp what made him so gay. But now I know.

He was so happy over the genesis of a new undertaking that would be good for Moscow. He was happy because some ray of light was to be brought into the dark lives of the poorer classes. All his life he was made happy by anything that brought beauty into human lives.

"Listen! But this is wonderful!" he used to say to me on such occasions, and a childishly bright smile on his face made him seem younger.

It was in the spring of the year 1897 that the Moscow Art and Popular Theatre was born. It was very difficult to drum up shareholders as this new undertaking did not promise success.

Anton Chekhov responded to the very first appeal and joined the group of shareholders. He was interested in every minute detail of our preparatory work and begged us to write in more detail and more frequently about it.

He was anxious to get to Moscow but his illness kept him anchored in Yalta which he nicknamed Devil's Island and compared himself to Dreyfus.

More than anything else it was, of course, the repertory of the future theatre that interested him. But for nothing in the world would he agree to have his *Seagull* produced. After its failure in St. Petersburg it was his crippled, and hence his favourite child. Nevertheless in August of 1898 *The Seagull* was included in the list of productions. I do not know how Nemirovich-Danchenko achieved this.

I went down to the country in the province of Kharkov to write out the production, the *mise-en-scène*.

It was a difficult project because I, to my shame, did not fully grasp the play. It was only in the course of working on it that imperceptibly I found my way into it, and unconsciously became enamoured of it. That is the characteristic of all Chekhov plays. Once you have yielded yourself to their enchantment you long to breathe deeply of all their fragrance.

I soon learned from letters that Chekhov had not been able to resist coming to Moscow. He probably came to follow the rehearsals of *The Seagull* which were beginning at that time. He was very much wrought up. By the time I returned he was no longer in Moscow. The bad weather had driven him back to Yalta. The rehearsals on *The Seagull* were temporarily halted.

Also when I returned the agitating days of the opening of the Art Theatre and the early months of its existence had commenced.

The business of the theatre was bad. Except for *Tsar Fyodor* which played to full houses, nothing drew the public. All our hopes were pinned on the Gerhard Hauptmann play *Hannele's Himmelfahrt,* but the Metropolitan Vladimir of Moscow found it censorable so he removed it from the repertory.

Our position reached a state of crisis, the more so because we did not look for material success from *The Seagull*. Yet we had to stage it. And everyone sensed that the fate of the theatre hinged on this production.

Nor was that all. On the eve of the opening night, just after a rather unsuccessful dress rehearsal Chekhov's sister Maria appeared at the theatre. She was very much exercised over bad news she had received from Yalta. The very thought of a second failure with *The Seagull* made her tremble for its effect on her brother's precarious health, and she could not be reconciled to the risks we were running.

We too were alarmed and even spoke of postponing the play, although that would have been tantamount to closing the theatre. It was not easy to contemplate signing the death sentence of one's own creation and condemning the whole company to hardship. And what of the shareholders? What would they say? Our responsibility to them was all too obvious.

The next day at eight in the evening the curtains were drawn. The audience was not numerous. How the first act went, I cannot say. All I know is that all the actors reeked of valerian drops. I can remember that I was terrified sitting there in the dim light with my back to the audience during Nina's monologue and that I unobtrusively held my leg which was nervously twitching.

It seemed as though we had failed completely. The curtains were closed amid a sepulchral silence. The actors looked furtively at each other and listened to the public.

The sepulchral silence continued.

The stage technicians came from the wings and they too listened. Silence.

Someone began to cry softly. Knipper stifled an hysterical sob. We began to move without a word towards the wings.

At that moment something like a sob came from the audience, followed by applause. The stage hands rushed to open the curtains.

They say that we were standing there, half turned away from the public, that our faces were terrible to see, that no one had the presence of mind to bow and that some of us actually remained seated. Obviously we had no idea what was going on.

The success we had had with the public was tremendous. Everybody kissed everybody else, even perfect strangers who forced their way backstage. Someone writhed on the floor in a fit of hysteria. Many, among them I myself, were so overjoyed that they threw themselves into a wild dance.

At the end of the performance the audience shouted for a congratulatory telegram to be sent to the absent author.

From that evening our relations with Anton Chekhov were on an almost family basis.

Our first season came to an end, spring was beginning, the trees were turning green. After the swallows Anton Chekhov came north again. He settled down in a small apartment belonging to his sister Maria. . . .

There was a simple wooden table in the middle of the room,

a simple inkwell, a pen, a pencil, a soft sofa, several chairs, a trunk full of books and notes—in short there was nothing except the necessities, nothing superfluous. This was the usual set-up for his improvised study while he was travelling.

In time the room would be filled with sketches by young painters, always talented, moving in new directions, oriented towards simplicity. The theme of these pictures was most often of the simplest nature—a Russian landscape in the style of Levitan—a few birds, a stream, a country house, etc.

Chekhov did not like frames so these sketches were usually fastened to the wall with thumb tacks.

Soon the writing table would be covered with slim notebooks. There were many of these. About this time Chekhov was occupied with correcting proofs of his already forgotten short stories written in his earliest period. He was preparing a new volume of these stories for his publisher Marx. As he renewed his acquaintance with them he laughed good-humouredly and his rich baritone voice would fill the whole apartment.

In the next room a samovar was often steaming and people rotated around the tea table kaleidoscope fashion; some came in as others went out. Among those who came often and sat there longest were the late painter Levitan, Bunin the writer, Nemirovich-Danchenko, Vishnevski, an actor in our theatre, Sulerzhitski and many others.

Among them there was usually a silent man or woman whom scarcely anyone knew. That would be some admirer, or a writer from Siberia, or a neighbour from an estate near his, a schoolmate, a childhood friend whom even his host did not recognize.

These people embarrassed everyone and particularly Chekhov himself but he made great use of a right he had earned: to disappear. From behind the door his guests would hear him coughing or listen to his measured steps up and down the room. Everyone was accustomed to these disappearances and knew that if a group of more congenial people came to the house he would appear more often and even sit with them, staring through his pince-nez at the silent figure of the uninvited guest. He was incapable of refusing to receive such a guest, much less able to hint that he was outstaying his welcome. Moreover Chekhov would get angry if anyone did this for him, although he would grin with satisfaction if that other person successfully manoeuvred the unwelcome guest out of the house. If such a stranger really stayed too long Chekhov would sometimes open his door a crack and beckon to one of his close friends to come into his bedroom. "Listen," he would say in an emphatic whisper, holding the door ever so slightly ajar with a firm hand, "you must tell him I don't know him, that I never went to high school. He has a novel in his pocket, I know he has. He'll stay to dinner, and afterwards he will read aloud from it. . . . This is impossible. . . . Listen. . . ."

Whenever the doorbell rang, and Chekhov did not like this, he would sit down on the sofa, keep still and try not to cough. A silence would fall on the whole apartment, the guests there would stop talking or hide in corners so that when the door would be opened no one would guess there were any people in the place at all.

One would hear the rustle of Maria's skirts, the sound of the chain on the door being unfastened, two voices in conversation.

"He is busy?" an unknown voice exclaims.

A long pause.

"A-ha, I see!" comes from the same voice.

"Just arrived—just for two minutes. . . ."

"Very well, I'll give the message."

"Only a short story . . . a play . . ." adds the voice of the stranger persuadingly.

"Goodbye," says Chekhov's sister.

"My profound, profound respects. . . . The expert opinion of such a man . . ."

"Yes, yes, I'll give the message," said in Maria's firm tones.

"The encouragement of young talents.... They must have enlightened patrons."

"Absolutely. Goodbye." This is said even more amiably.

"Oh, excuse me!" is followed by the thud of a parcel, the rustle of papers, the sound of rubbers being pulled on, then again, "Goodbye ... my deepest ... most profound ... overflowing with ... such esthetic ... my most profound ... moved to the depths of my being ..."

Finally the door closes and Maria Chekhov lays on the writing table several untidy manuscripts tied up with a ravelled cord.

"Tell them I'm not doing any more writing ... one really shouldn't write," Chekhov would say as he eyed the manuscripts.

Nevertheless he not only read these manuscripts but sent a reply to their authors.

You must not think that when we met after the success of *The Seagull* there was anything affecting about our encounter. He shook my hand more firmly than usual, smiled pleasantly—that was all. Chekhov was not in favour of expansive expression, whereas I felt a strong urge towards it since I had become his ardent admirer. I found it difficult to establish a simple relationship with him, such as I had had formerly, because now I felt very small in the presence of a famous person. I wished I were bigger, more intelligent than God had made me, so I deliberately chose words and attempted to talk about important subjects— indeed I reminded myself of a neurotic woman in the presence of her idol. Chekhov sensed this and was embarrassed by it. It was years before I could achieve the unaffected relation to him which was all he wanted to have with anyone.

Besides I was unable, at this meeting, to conceal the impression made on me by the fatal change that had come over him. His illness had left its cruel mark. Perhaps the look on my face alarmed him. In any case we found it difficult to remain alone together. Fortunately Nemirovich-Danchenko came in soon and we began to talk about theatre matters. These consisted of our wishing to obtain the rights to produce his play *Uncle Vanya*.

"Why do you want it.... You really shouldn't.... I'm not a playwright," was Chekhov's negative reply.

The worst of the situation was that the Imperial Maly Theatre was trying to do the same thing that we were. A. I. Yuzhin, the energetic defender of the interests of this theatre, was not asleep at his post.

In order to avoid the painful necessity of offending either of us by his refusal, Chekhov invented all sorts of reasons why he should not give his play to the one or the other of the theatres.

"I really must rewrite the play," he told Yuzhin, and to us he insisted: "I don't know your theatre. I have to see how you act."

A chance incident came to our rescue. Some official of the Imperial Theatre asked Chekhov to come for some negotiations. Of course it would have been more proper if this official had taken the bother to call on Chekhov.

Their conversation began in an extremely strange fashion. First of all the official put this question to the famous author:

"What is your occupation?"

"I write," replied Chekhov, astonished.

"That is to say ... yes, of course, I know that—but ... what do you write?" continued the muddled official.

Anton Chekhov reached for his hat and made a motion to leave.

Then His Excellency made a further unsuccessful attempt to come to the point. This was that the Committee on Repertory had examined *Uncle Vanya* and was not in accord with the shooting in the third act. It would be necessary to rewrite the ending. In the report the following, unexplained motives of the committee were stated more or less in these words: it cannot be conceded that anyone should shoot at a university professor, a person who had received a diploma.

After this statement Chekhov bowed and left, requesting that a copy of this remarkable report be sent to him. He showed it to us with undisguised indignation.

After this comic-dramatic event the question of the play solved itself. Nonetheless Chekhov stubbornly repeated:

"I do not know your theatre."

This was really slyness on his part. He simply wanted to see *The Seagull* in our production. So we gave him an opportunity to do so.

As we had no permanent quarters our company was temporarily housed at the Nikitski Theatre. It was there that we put on a performance without an audience. It was there that all our sets were carried. The surroundings of a dusty, empty, ill-lighted, damp theatre, with props carried in for the occasion, were not likely to inspire actors to perform for their single spectator. Nevertheless the performance pleased Chekhov. Probably he had been homesick for the theatre during his "exile" in Yalta.

With almost childish glee he walked around on the stage, inspected the dirty dressing rooms of the actors. He loved the theatre not only on its showy side but on its seamy side as well.

He was delighted with the performance as a whole but objected to some of the performers. He criticized me, for instance, in the role of Trigorin.

"You act magnificently," he said, "but not my character. I did not write that."

"What's the matter with it?" I asked.

"Why, he should have checked trousers and worn-out shoes." That was all he would say in reply to my urgent questioning.

"Checked trousers . . . and this is how he smokes a cigar. . . ." Here he awkwardly explained his words in gestures.

That was how he always made his remarks: vividly and briefly. They always astonished and impressed themselves on the memory of those concerned. Chekhov really gave us charades which we could not put out of our minds until we solved them.

It was only six years later that I guessed my charade, when we revived *The Seagull*.

As a matter of fact why did I play Trigorin like a dandy in white trousers and fancy beach slippers? Could it have been because I was in love with that image of him? Was such a costume really typical of a Russian literary figure? Of course, the point was not in the checked trousers, worn shoes and the cigar. Nina Zarechnaya, having read the nice but vapid short stories of Trigorin, falls in love not with him but with her own girlish dream. There is the tragedy of the gull he shoots. There too is the mockery and harshness of life. When a country girl is in love for the first time she does not notice the loud checked trousers, nor the worn shoes, nor the evil-smelling cigar. One sees these monstrosities of life much later on, when life itself is broken, when all the sacrifices have been made, and love has become a habit. Then one must find new illusions, for one must go on living—and Nina seeks for them in faith.

But I have wandered from my story. Chekhov was brutally critical of the way one of the parts was played. One could hardly have expected such comments from such an exceptionally mild man. He insisted indeed that the role be taken from the actor without delay. He refused to accept any excuses and threatened to forbid further performances of the play.

While discussing other parts he would allow a certain lightness in describing inadequacies, but the moment the conversation returned to this one role he promptly changed his tone and speaking like a merciless sledge hammer he said:

"It cannot be, listen—you have a serious undertaking here."

That was the point which made him unrelenting.

Those were the words too which explained his attitude towards our theatre. He never gave us any compliments, nor detailed criticisms, nor encouragement.

Because the weather was mild Chekhov spent the spring of this year in Moscow and he attended our rehearsals every day.

He did not participate in our work. He merely enjoyed being in the atmosphere of art and chatting with jolly actors. He loved the theatre, but he could not tolerate any triviality in it. It made him cringe to a morbid degree, or run away where he could not see it.

"I have to go, excuse me, people are waiting for me," he would say, and go home, sit down on his sofa and sink into thought.

A few days later, almost like some reflex action he would bring out an unexpected phrase which would contain a sharp summing up of the triviality which had so upset him.

"I object on *prrrrinciple*," he announced once and they rocked with laughter for some time. He had remembered the incredibly long speech of a pseudo-Russian character who talked about the poetry of the Russian countryside and used this phrase.

We, of course, took every opportunity to talk about *Uncle Vanya,* but to our questions all Chekhov would answer was:

"It's all written in it."

Nevertheless he did once make a definite statement. Someone mentioned a production of *Uncle Vanya* he had seen in the provinces. In it the title part was taken by a man who played him as a gone-to-seed landowner, in greasy boots and a peasant blouse. That was the way Russian landowners were always represented on the stage.

Good God—what that did to Chekhov!

"No, not that, listen . . . I wrote: he wears marvelous neckties. Marvelous ones! Remember, landowners dress better than you or I."

Of course the case in point was not the necktie but the central idea of the play. The "native" Astrov and poetic, tender Uncle Vanya are going to seed in the depths of the country, while the blockhead of a professor takes his ease in St. Petersburg and he and others like him rule Russia.

That is the thought behind the necktie. . . .

In 1899 *Uncle Vanya* was a great success. As soon as the play was over the audience insisted on "a telegram to Chekhov!"

Judging by his letters Chekhov all winter long nursed the hopes of a trip to Moscow. He was by now warmly attached to our theatre which he had never seen in action, unless you count the improvised performance of *The Seagull*.

He was thinking about writing a play for us.

"But in order to do that I must see your theatre," he kept asserting in his letters.

When it became clear that his doctors had forbidden the spring journey to Moscow we took his hint and decided to take the whole production to Yalta.

In April 1900 the entire company and their families, the sets and props for four plays left Moscow for Sevastopol. Others, devoted followers of Chekhov and of our theatre, joined us and even one critic, S. V. Vassiliev (Flerov) went along. He made the journey just for the purpose of writing detailed accounts of our performances.

It was a great migration of peoples. On this journey I recall especially A. R. Artem who left his wife for the first time. Feeling helpless, he picked himself a "companion" for the trip, his fellow actor A. L. Vishnevski, who became temporarily the fountainhead of his energy and will power. As we were nearing Sevastopol, Artem kept asking us all if there were any cabs to be had, or did we have to go on foot up into the hills, etc.

Very often when Vishnevski had been absent for some time Artem would send for him. All the way Artem talked about death and was very gloomy.

Near Sevastopol, where there are some tunnels, great rocks and beautiful sights, the whole company poured out onto the platforms of the train. Even gloomy Artem, convoyed by Vishnevski, came out for the first time. Vishnevski with his characteristically buoyant temperament kept consoling Artem: "No, no, Sasha, you aren't going to die! Why should you die? Look, see the gulls, the sea, the rocks! No, you aren't going to die, Sasha!"

Then under the influence of the rocks, the sea, the beautiful winding road along which the train was swiftly moving, the artist in Artem was aroused, he began to look with gleaming eyes at the sights all around him. Suddenly he shook his head and looking crossly at Vishnevski said in a rather insidious way:

"Who said I would die? Why would I want to!" and then turning away he added, with some annoyance,

"Whatever were you inventing!"

The Crimea received us without warmth. An icy wind was blowing in from the sea, the sky was overcast, there was some means of heating the hotels but still we froze.

The theatre was still boarded up since the winter, a storm tore down our posters which no one read.

Our spirits sank.

But then the sun came out, the sea smiled at us and we cheered up.

Some people came, took down the shutters, opened the doors. We entered. It was cold as a cellar inside. It was indeed a basement which it would take over a week to air out and we had to perform in it in two to three days. What upset me most was the thought of Chekhov and how he could sit in that musty atmosphere. The women in our group spent a whole day on choosing the best place for him to sit, where there would be the least draft. Our company began to congregate more and more around the theatre, things began to boil.

We were in a holiday mood—it was our second season, everyone blossomed out in new suits, hats, it was all very young in spirit and everyone was terribly pleased to be an actor. At the same time everyone made a great effort to be on his best behaviour, because after all we were not some whistle-stop company but a troupe from the capital.

Finally an elaborately dressed lady put in an appearance. She announced that she was of the local aristocracy, a friend of Chek-

97

hov, and demanded a box for all performances. After her swarmed the public and very soon all the tickets for the four performances had been sold.

We were waiting for Chekhov. For the time being Olga Knipper, who had been given leave to go to Yalta, was not writing to us from there, and this disturbed us very much. On Easter Saturday she returned with the sad news that Chekhov had been taken ill and it was scarcely probable that he would be able to come to Sevastopol.

This saddened us all. From her we learned that it was much warmer in Yalta (that was what one always heard), that Chekhov was a remarkable man and also that practically all the representatives of Russian literature were gathered there: Gorki, Mamin-Siberyak, Stanyukovich, Bunin, Elpatievski, Naidenov, Skitalets.

That agitated us even more.

Then we went out to buy the traditional Easter food—paskha, kulich—to be eaten now at the end of Lent and far from home.

At midnight the bells tolled, but not as they did in Moscow, nor was the singing the same, and even the Easter food smacked of Turkish delight.

Artem was highly critical of Sevastopol, having decided that one can celebrate Easter only at home. However, a walk along the sea after the breaking of the Great Fast and the early morning air of Spring made us forget about the North. At dawn it was so wonderful that we began to sing gypsy songs and recite verse to the pounding waves.

The next day we waited impatiently for the arrival of the steamer which was to bring Chekhov. Finally we saw him. He was the last to emerge from the cabin companion-way, pale and thin, and coughing badly. His eyes were sad and full of illness but he tried to smile a greeting.

I wanted to weep.

Our amateur photographers snapped pictures of him as he left the ship and this little scene of picture-taking was incorporated in the play he was then carrying in his head (*The Three Sisters*).

With a general absence of tact we flooded him with questions about his health.

"It's fine. I am quite well," he kept replying.

He did not like any fuss made over his health, not from strangers, nor even from close friends. He never complained no matter how ill he felt.

Soon he went to his hotel and we left him alone until the next day. He was not stopping where we were. Probably he was afraid of being so near the sea.

The next day, Easter Monday, our performances began. We faced a double test, in front of Anton Chekhov, and a new audience.

The whole day passed in a state of turmoil and business.

I saw Chekhov only for an instant in the theatre. He came to look over his box. He was concerned with two things: would he be shielded from the public and where was the box of that "lady-aristocrat"?

Despite the severe cold he was wearing a light overcoat. A lot was said about that but again he remarked tersely:

"Listen! I'm quite well!"

There was a chill in the theatre because the walls were cracked and there was no heating. The dressing rooms were warmed by kerosene lamps. . . .

In the evening we all put on our make-up in one small dressing room which we heated by the warmth of our own bodies but the actresses who had to make a show in their muslin dresses ran across to the hotel; there they warmed themselves and changed their costumes.

At eight o'clock a shrill hand-bell called the audience to the first performance—*Uncle Vanya*.

The dark figure of the author, concealed behind Nemirovich-Danchenko and his wife in the management box put our feelings on edge.

The first act was received coolly but at the end the applause turned into a great ovation. The audience called for the author. He was in despair but nevertheless made an appearance.

The next day Artem was so emotionally exhausted that he kept to his bed and did not appear at rehearsal. Chekhov, who loved to practice as a doctor was delighted as soon as he heard about Artem; he was to have a patient, and a patient of whom he was particularly fond. He and Tikhomirov started off at once to see the sick man. We were all agog to hear what Chekhov would prescribe and how he would treat Artem. On his way to him Chekhov, curiously enough, stopped by his hotel to pick up a little hammer and a piece of pipe.

"Listen, I can't go there without any instruments," he said in a worried tone.

He sounded his patient at length, thumped him, and was finally convinced that he was not in need of any treatment. He gave him a piece of some sort of mint candy and said:

"Here now, listen, eat this!"

This was the end of the treatment. Next day Artem had recovered and appeared at rehearsal.

Chekhov liked to come when we were rehearsing but as it was extremely cold inside he would just look in occasionally and mostly spend his time sitting in the sun in a small place in front of the theatre where the actors liked to warm themselves in the sunlight.

"Listen, this is a marvellous thing, a remarkable thing—your theatre."

That was, you might say, a popular saying with Chekhov at that time. What usually went on was that Chekhov would be sitting out in front of the theatre in an excited, gay mood, chatting with the actors and actresses especially, Olga Knipper and Maria Andreyeva, to both of whom he was paying court, and using every opportunity to say unpleasant things about Yalta. In this there were tragic overtones.

"In winter the sea is black there, black as ink . . ."

Occasionally he would let slip a phrase showing great fatigue and sadness.

It was here, I remember, that he spent several hours with a stage carpenter showing him how to reproduce the sound of a cricket.

"He chirps," he would say as he demonstrated it, "then for so many seconds he is silent. Then again he goes: chirp, chirp."

At a certain time a Mr. N. would appear in the little square in front of the theatre and begin to talk about literature, saying all the wrong things. Chekhov would immediately, imperceptibly freeze up.

The next day, after the performance of Hauptmann's *Lonely Lives* which made a most powerful impression on him, Chekhov said:

"What a marvellous play!"

He used to say what an important thing in life the theatre was, and that one really must write for the theatre.

As far as I recall the first time he said this was after *Lonely Lives*. Among other things discussed in front of the theatre was *Uncle Vanya*—he was full of praise for everyone in the cast and he made only one remark to me about Astrov in the last act.

"Listen, he whistles. It is Uncle Vanya who whimpers but Astrov whistles."

With my inflexible way of looking at things in those days I could not reconcile myself to this idea—how could a person in such a dramatic situation whistle?

He always arrived long ahead of time for the performance. He loved to come on stage, and watch the scenery being set up. In the intermissions he went from dressing room to dressing room and talked all sorts of nonsense to the actors. He always adored all the little details of theatrical life—how sets were let down, how the lighting worked, and when such matters were talked about in front of him he would stand there and smile happily.

When we were playing *Hedda Gabler* he often came to our dressing rooms and would stay even after the next act began. This upset us—it must mean he did not like the performance, since he did not hurry back to his place out front. And when we asked him about this he quite unexpectedly burst out:

"Listen, Ibsen is no playwright!"

Chekhov did not see *The Seagull* in Sevastopol—he had already seen it and the weather turned bad, the wind rose, there were storms, he felt worse and was forced to leave.

The performance of *The Seagull* was given under terrible conditions. The wind was so strong that a stagehand had to stand behind each wing and hold it up so it would not topple over toward the audience with every gust of wind.

All through the performance we heard the alarm signals blown from ships and the shriek of sirens. Our clothing waved around in the wind which swept the stage. It poured rain outside.

Then there was another incident: in order to get the necessary power to light the stage the current had to be diverted from half of the city park. We felt it was impossible to give up this lighting effect. This was one of the Nemirovich-Danchenko's moments of decision—he simply gave orders to put the lights out in one half of the city park.

The Seagull was a tremendous success. After the performance the public crowded around us. As I came out down some small steps with an umbrella in my hand I was grabbed, I think by a group of high-school girls. But they could not get control of me. I was in a pitiable state; they yelled at me, took hold of one of my feet so I had to hop on the other because they were dragging me forward, my umbrella flew off, the rain came down in sheets, but it was not possible to offer any explanations as everyone was yelling "Hurrah!" My wife ran after me and was frantic thinking I might be crippled. Fortunately their strength soon gave out, they let me go, so that by the time I got to the hotel I was walking on both of my feet. But at the very entrance they tried to do something else to me and succeeded in stretching me full length on the muddy steps.

The porter came out and began to wipe me off, but the girls, who were all out of breath, still raged around and argued about what had happened and why.

We knew all the authorities of Sevastopol and before we left for Yalta they were giving us telephonic weather reports: "Northwest, Northeast, there will be pitching, there will be no pitching." All the sailors said the crossing would be smooth, that the rough place would be near Ai-Todor, then after that we would come into smooth water.

But actually there was no turn for the better and we were shaken up so badly we shall never forget it.

We were really shaken to pieces on the way. Many of us were travelling with our wives and children. Some of the people from Sevastopol travelled with us to Yalta. Nurses, maids, children, scenery, props, everything was stowed on the deck of the steamer. In Yalta there was a crowd waiting on the pier, with flowers, all dressed in their Sunday best; the sea raged, the wind howled. It was complete chaos.

Yet we were having a new sensation, the feeling that the crowds recognized us. We felt the joy and embarrassment of our new situation, it was the first flush of popularity.

We had scarcely arrived at Yalta and had time to get to our rooms, wash up and look around, when I met Vishnevski, who arrived on the run breathless with excitement, yelling and shouting, quite beside himself:

"I've just met Gorki—what a charmer! He has already decided to write a play for us! Without even seeing us act. . . ."

The next morning the first thing I did was to go to the theatre. I found they were taking down partitions, cleaning up, scrubbing, in fact working at top speed. Strolling around amid the shavings and dust I found Gorki, carrying a cane, Bunin, Mirolyubov, Mamin-Sibiryak, Elpatievski, Nemirovich-Danchenko.

After looking over the stage the whole group went off to the city park [restaurant] to lunch. Immediately the entire terrace there was swarming with our actors and we occupied the whole park. Stanyukovich sat at a little table by himself. Somehow he did not fit in with the crowd.

From there the entire crowd, some on foot, some in groups of six or in carriages, set off for Chekhov's home. His table was always laid either for a little meal or for tea. His house was not yet finished, there was a scraggly little garden around it which he had only just set out.

Chekhov looked extremely lively, really transformed as though he had risen from the dead. I recall exactly the impression he made—it was that of a house which having been locked up for winter, with all the shutters closed, now in the Spring was opened up, light streaming into all the rooms which smiled and sparkled in the sun. He kept moving from place to place, his hands clasped behind his back or else forever adjusting his pince-nez. One moment he was out on the terrace, which was strewn with new books and magazines, the next he was down in the garden with a constant smile on his face, or in the courtyard. Only rarely did he disappear into his study and apparently take a little rest.

People kept arriving and leaving. When one meal was finished the next was served. Maria Chekhov was worn out, Olga Knipper, like a true friend (or perhaps as the future mistress of the household) had rolled up her sleeves and was doing what she could to be of help.

In one corner a literary discussion would be going on, in the garden a group would be throwing stones like schoolboys to see who could throw farthest, in a third place Ivan Bunin, with extraordinary talent, would be acting out something. And wherever Bunin was Chekhov was bound to be, roaring with laughter, in fact doubled up with it. No one could make Chekhov laugh as Bunin did when he was in a good mood.

For me the centre of attraction was Gorki who had instantly enslaved me with his charm. His unusual figure, face, pronunciation, strange gestures, his balled fist in moments of excitement, the bright, childlike smile on a face sometimes steeped in tragic expression, his amusing or powerful, eloquent, vivid speech—all this radiated a kind of spiritual softness and grace; despite the stoop in his carriage there was a special kind of plasticity and external beauty in his form. I often found myself admiring a pose of his or a gesture.

Then too the loving look that was in his eyes so often when they rested on Chekhov, the smile that spread over his face at the slightest sound of Chekhov's voice, the good-natured way he laughed at even the slightest joke made by Chekhov, somehow drew us together in a common bond of affection for our host.

Chekhov, who loved to talk of his infatuations of the moment, went around like a naïve child asking everyone the same question: had this or that guest seen our theatre?

"It's a marvellous thing! You really must write a play for this theatre."

And without letup he said over and over again what a magnificent play *Lonely Lives* was.

Gorki with his tales of nomadic life, Mamin-Sibiryak with his bold humour which sometimes assumed the proportions of buffoonery, Bunin with his exquisite wit, Chekhov with his unexpected rejoinders, Moskvin with his keen sallies—all this created an inspiriting atmosphere which welded us into a single family of artists. We all had the same idea of getting together in Yalta, we even talked of arranging for a place. In short, it was the Spring, sea, gaiety, youth, poetry and art, which combined to make the atmosphere in which we found ourselves at that time. And these afternoon and evening gatherings were repeated nearly every day at the home of Anton Chekhov.

A mixed crowd milled around the box office of the theatre: there were elegantly dressed ladies and their escorts from the two capital cities [St. Petersburg and Moscow], teachers, officials from a variety of provincial cities all over Russia, local inhabitants, consumptive patients, who during their depressed winters had not forgotten the existence of art.

Our first performance ended most successfully with floral tributes and all sorts of gifts. And this despite the fact that the Municipal Orchestra in the city park provided a loud accompaniment of a polka or a military march even during the tragic passages of our play.

In the city park, on the terrace, hot arguments took place about the new tendencies in art, new literature. Some, even of the outstanding writers, did not have even an elementary conception of realistic art, others went off in a diametrically opposite direction and dreamed of seeing things on the stage that were utterly unworthy of it. In any case our performances stirred animated discussions, which almost went as far as physical violence and therefore achieved their purpose. All the writers present suddenly seemed to be reminded of the existence of the theatre; some of them secretly and others quite openly began to think in terms of plays.

The thing that ruined Chekhov's pleasure in our performances was that he had to go out and take bows in response to the clamour of the audience. He received an almost daily ovation. Because of this he sometimes dropped out of sight suddenly and then someone had to go out in front of the curtain and explain that the playwright was not in the theatre. But mostly he just came backstage and strolled from dressing room to dressing room, enjoying backstage life, its tremendous excitements, its successes and failures, which gave him an even keener sense of life.

In the mornings we all gathered on the quay. I stuck close to Gorki and as we walked along he would toy with various ideas for a play. These talks were constantly interrupted by the pranks of his very lively little boy Maxim, who was incessantly up to the most unlikely enterprises.

There is one other incident which stands out in my recollection of this stay in Yalta. One day I went to see Chekhov and found him truculent, fierce and bristling—in other words in a state in which I had never seen him. When he had quieted down the explanation came out. His mother, whom he idolized, had finally prepared herself to go and see *Uncle Vanya*. For this aged lady this was an absolutely exceptional occasion—just think she was going to see a play by her "Antosha." She began to get ready very early in the day. She went through all her trunks and at the bottom of one of them she found an old-fashioned silk dress which she planned to wear on this solemn occasion. Accidentally her plan was discovered by her son and he began to be all upset. He imagined this picture: the son has written a play and his mamma is sitting there with a silk dress on in a box. This sentimental picture so unstrung him that he wanted to take the train to Moscow rather than be part of the occasion.

In the evenings we sometimes gathered in a private dining room in the Hotel Rossiya. Someone would play on the piano; it was all very amateurish and naïve, nevertheless the sounds of it kept fresh floods of tears coming to Gorki's eyes.

One evening Gorki was somehow carried away and told us about the subject of the play he proposed to write. It was to be laid in a poor lodging house, stuffy atmosphere, wooden bunks, during a long monotonous winter. The people had been bestialized by the hideousness of their existence, they had lost patience and hope, and being depleted of patience they nag each other, talk philosophy. Each one tries to prove to the others he is still a human being. Some sort of former waiter is especially vain of his cheap cotton shirt front—the only remaining vestige of his former dress suit life. One of the inmates of the lodgings, in order to rile the waiter, steals his dickie and tears it in two. The former waiter finds the pieces of his torn shirt front and because of it raises a most frightful row. He is full of despair because the destruction of his dickie tears away the last remaining contact with his former life. The swearing and brawling goes on late into the night, and is stopped by the word of an impending visit from the police on the beat. There are hasty preparations to meet the police, they all run around and hide whatever is of value or might be compromising. They all stretch out on the wooden bunks and pretend to be asleep. The police come. One person without identification papers is hauled off to the police station and sleep enfolds the bunks; only one old pilgrim climbs down in the silence from the bunk above the [great brick] stove, takes the stub of a candle out of his sack, lights it and begins to pray with fervour. A Tatar sticks his head out from one of the bunks and says:

"Pray for me!"

That is the end of the first act.

The succeeding acts were only vaguely sketched so that it was hard to follow the action. In the last act it is Spring and sunny. The lodgers are digging in the earth. The weary creatures have come out of doors into Nature's holiday and they seem to have come alive. Under the influence of Nature they seem to love one another. That is the way I recall all that Gorki told me about his play.

The company finished its series of productions and our stay was topped off by a marvellous luncheon party on the great flat roof of Fanny Tatarinova's house. I remember the hot day, some sort of gay awning and the sparkling sea in the distance. The whole company had gathered there, and all the world of literature, so to say, with Chekhov and Gorki at the head of it, and also the wives and children.

I remember the enthusiastic speeches, warmed by the southern sun, full of hope, infinite hope.

This marvellous holiday under the open sky brought our stay in Yalta to a close.

The following year our repertory included: *The Snow Maiden, The Enemy of Society, The Three Sisters, When We Dead Awake.*

From the very start of the season Chekhov sent frequent letters on this or that subject. He begged us all to send him news of the theatre. These little notes of Chekhov, his constant attention imperceptibly influenced our theatre very deeply, although we did not quite appreciate this until after his death.

He was interested in every little detail and especially, of course, in the repertory of the theatre. And we were always egging him on to write a play. From his letters we gathered that he was writing a play, that it had to do with army life and that some regiment or other went somewhere or other. But we could not guess from the brief and random phrases he let drop what the real subject of the play was.

In his letters as in his writings he was niggardly with words. The random phrases, the little clusters of his creative thoughts could be appreciated only when we came to know the play itself.

Either he was stuck in his writing or the play had long since been written and he was unwilling to let it go out of his hands but was making it lie there on his desk—whatever the reason he kept postponing its dispatch to us. As an alibi he kept assuring us that there were so many fine plays in the world that we should put on Hauptmann, Hauptmann should write more, and that he himself was not a playwright, etc., etc.

All these excuses filled us with despair, we wrote imploring letters, to hurry and send the play and save the theatre, etc. We were not aware at the time that we were using force on the creativeness of a great artist.

Finally one or two acts of the play arrived, written in the familiar fine handwriting. We read them voraciously but, as always happens with any real writing for the stage, its principal beauties did not appear in our reading of it. With only two acts in our hands we could not work out stage sets, assign roles, nor begin any preparatory work for the production. So we tried by means of more energetic measures to get the other two acts. We finally succeeded but not without a struggle.

In the end Chekhov agreed to send the play, he even brought it to us in person.

He never read his own plays aloud, so it was with considerable embarrassment and agitation that he listened to its first reading to the company. When this began and Chekhov was appealed to for explanations he was terribly embarrassed and kept refusing to say anything except:

"Listen, I wrote it all down. Everything I knew."

As a matter of fact he never was able to criticize his own plays and he always listened to the opinions of others with interest and astonishment. The things that astonished him most and with which he, to the day of his death, could not agree was that his *Three Sisters* (and later *The Cherry Orchard*) was a serious drama of Russian life. He was sincerely convinced that it was a gay comedy, almost a farce. I cannot remember that he ever defended his own opinion about anything as hotly as he did when at the reading for the first time he heard others speak of his play in such terms.

Of course we took advantage of the presence of the author to extract from him certain necessary details. But even then his replies were monosyllabic. At the time they were obscure and incomprehensible to us, and it was only later that we realized how extraordinarily vivid in imagery they were and felt how typical they were of him and his plays.

When we began our preparatory work (on *The Three Sisters*) Chekhov insisted that we call in a general who was an acquaintance of his. He wanted the military details to be reproduced with absolute accuracy. Chekhov himself acted like a complete outsider, taking no part at all in our work, merely observing it.

He was unable to help us in our work, our searchings for the true inwardness of the Prozorov household. We felt that he knew it himself in detail, had been there, but had taken absolutely no note of what rooms there were, or furniture, or objects contained in them—in other words, he felt only the atmosphere of each room separately but not its walls.

That is how a writer senses the life about him. But that is not enough for the person directing a play, who has to determine things exactly and then order all the details reproduced.

Now we can understand why Chekhov grinned happily and laughed with such good nature when what the scene designer and director did coincided with his own conceptions. He studied at length and in greatest detail the models of the sets and then roared with good-humoured laughter. One has to have a certain amount of experience to judge what a model will look like when it materializes on the stage. This is a theatrical, a "scene-sense," and Anton Chekhov had it, just as by nature he was a "theatre man." He loved, he understood, he really felt the theatre—of course in its best aspect. He loved to tell about how he used to act in various plays when he was young and told amusing stories about the rehearsals for these amateur productions. He loved the excited atmosphere of rehearsals and performance, loved the work of the stage crews, he loved to soak up all the little details of stage life and techniques; and above all he was particularly keen on true-to-life noises on the stage.

One of the things he was most concerned about in connection with the play (*The Three Sisters*) was how the fire alarm in the third act would be handled. He wanted to have the real flavour of the clanging fire bell in a small town. On every available occasion he would come up to one or the other of us and use his hands, beat rhythms, gesticulate, in order to instill in us the mood induced by the soul-searing sound of the fire bell in a provincial town.

He was present at nearly every rehearsal of his play but only very seldom did he proffer an opinion and even then he did it cautiously, almost fearfully. There was only one thing he insisted upon with particular vehemence: as in *Uncle Vanya* he feared that in this play there might be a danger of caricaturing provincial life, of showing the army men as routine theatrical stuffed shirts with clanking spurs, instead of playing them as simple, nice, good people, dressed in worn-out theatrical uniforms, without any special military carriage, high shoulders, abrupt manners, etc.

"All that doesn't exist," he insisted with some warmth, "the army people have changed, they are more cultured, many of them are even beginning to realize that in peace-time they must carry culture with them into the out-of-the-way places where they are stationed."

He was all the more insistent on this because the army, having gotten wind of the fact that a play had been written about their way of life was quite agitated.

The rehearsals took place in the presence of the general Chekhov had recommended. He became so interested in the theatre and exercised over the fate of the play that he often forgot his special assignment and became much more excited over whether this or that actor was handling his role or a certain situation properly.

Chekhov studied the whole repertory of our theatre and made his usual laconic remarks which were couched in such unexpected terms that they made you puzzle over them as you could not always understand them at once. It was only after some time had elapsed that you could really absorb them. It was the sort of thing I mentioned earlier when he remarked that in the last act of *Uncle Vanya,* in a tragic situation, Astrov begins to whistle.

Chekhov was not able to stay for the dress rehearsal of *The Three Sisters.* His health declined and forced him to go to a warmer climate, so he left for Nice.

From there we received little notes—in such and such a scene, after such and such words, "insert this phrase." For example: "Balzac was married in Berdichev."

On another occasion he sent a little scene. All these little gems when studied during rehearsal put a lot of life into our work and stirred the actors to play with more sincere feelings.

We also had another piece of instruction from abroad. In the fourth act of *The Three Sisters* Andrei, who has let himself go, talks with Ferapont because no one else was willing to talk with him, and he describes what a wife is from the point of view of a provincial man who has gone to seed. He has a magnificent monologue two pages long. Then suddenly came the order to strike out the entire monologue and in its place put these five words, nothing more:

"A wife is a wife!"

If you think about it carefully you will find that this short phrase contains all that was said in the two pages of monologue. That was very characteristic of Chekhov; what he wrote was always succinct and compact. Each word of his was accompanied by a whole scale of varying moods and thoughts. He did not state them explicitly but they came to your mind of their own accord.

That is why I never played a performance even when I already had acted in his play a hundred times, without making fresh discoveries in the long-familiar text and the emotions of my part which I had been through so often. The depth of Chekhov's writings is inexhaustible for any thoughtful and sensitive actor.

How agitated Chekhov was about the opening of *The Three Sisters* can be judged by the fact that the day before it took place he left the town where we had his address and no one knew where he had gone, so that he could not be reached with the news of the play's fate.

Its success was equivocal.

After the first act there was ringing applause. The actors took about twelve curtain calls. After the second act there was only one curtain call. After the third act there was some half-hearted applause but not enough to allow the actors to take a curtain call and after the fourth act they bowed only once.

We had to do a considerable amount of inflating to wire Chekhov that the play was a "big success."

It was only three years after this first performance that the public finally came to appreciate all the beauty of this remarkable piece of writing, and they began to laugh or be quiet at the places the author intended. By then every act was a triumph.

The press too was very long in coming to a real appreciation of this play.

In Moscow the year the play was first produced, there were only a few performances, and then it was taken to St. Petersburg. Chekhov was expected to go there but bad weather and ill health prevented.

On returning to Moscow the theatre began preparations for its next season. Chekhov arrived. There was talk in the company of the possibility of his marrying Olga Knipper. It was true enough that they were seen often together.

One day Chekhov asked Vishnevski to invite all his (Chekhov's) relatives and for some reason also all of Olga Knipper's relatives on a certain date to dinner. The day came and all the guests were assembled. The only persons missing were Anton Chekhov and Olga Knipper. The guests waited, grew increasingly worried, became upset until finally they received word that Chekhov had taken Olga Knipper to church and married her and that from there they had immediately left for Samara to take the Kumyss cure.

The whole dinner had been planned in order to get all the persons out of the way who might have prevented an intimate marriage ceremony shorn of all the usual wedding fuss and feathers. The social activities connected with a wedding were extremely distasteful to Chekhov. From the train they sent a wire to Vishnevski.

The following year Chekhov arranged to spend the autumn in Moscow and go to Yalta only for the coldest months. And he actually did come to Moscow and spend some time there but somehow this is a period which has not remained very distinct in my memory. All I can recall are isolated incidents.

I remember for instance that Chekhov saw rehearsals of *The Wild Duck* and was obviously bored. He did not like Ibsen. He sometimes said:

"Listen, Ibsen doesn't know life. Things don't happen that way in life."

Nevertheless Chekhov never saw Artem in the play that he did not smile and he kept saying:

"I am going to write a play for him. He will have to sit on the shore of a river and be catching fish. . . ."

Then, after a pause, he would add:

". . . And Vishnevski will be bathing nearby, splashing and talking loudly . . ."

Then he would roar with laughter at the combination of the two.

One day at a rehearsal we began to urge him to write another play, and he began to hint at the subject he had in mind for one. He was thinking of an open window and a branch of white cherry blossoms coming through it from the orchard outside. Artem was already cast as a footman and then, for no reason, a steward. His master, or sometimes he thought it was his mistress, was always short of money, and at times of crisis appealed to the footman or steward for some because he had a considerable pile of savings somehow put aside.

After that Chekhov added a group of billiard players. One of them—an ardent player, was all thumbs, jolly, buoyant, always very loud in his speech. He seemed to see Vishnevski in this part. Later a conservatory was introduced which was then metamorphosed into a billiard room.

But all these fragments, through which he let us peep at his play, gave us no real idea of what it was to be, yet we spent our energies urging him to write it.

In inverse ratio to his dislike of Ibsen was his enthusiasm for

Hauptmann. At this time we were rehearsing *Michael Kramer* and Chekhov watched us closely.

A very characteristic trait of his nature—the immediate and naïve way he received impressions—has remained vividly in my memory.

At the dress rehearsal of the second act of *Michael Kramer* when I was on stage I could hear his ripples of laughter now and then. But since the action in progress on the stage was not such as to provoke such a reaction from the public, and since I valued Chekhov's opinion very highly, this laughter upset me very much. More than that, right in the middle of the action Chekhov left his place several times and walked rapidly along the centre aisle still laughing. That upset the actors still more.

At the end of the act I went out front to find out the cause of Chekhov's attitude and I found him beaming and still running up and down the aisle.

I asked him what he thought of the performance. He said he liked it very much.

"How good it is," he told us, "it's marvellous, you know, really marvellous."

It appeared that he was laughing from pleasure. Only the most unaffected people can laugh that way.

I can recall peasants, who can laugh at the most inappropriate places in a play out of sheer pleasure of seeing artistic truths.

"How true to life!" they always say.

It was during this season that Chekhov saw *The Three Sisters* and he was very well pleased with the production, although, in his opinion, the fire alarm in the third act was not successfully handled. He decided to arrange this sound himself. Obviously he wanted to experiment with the stagehands, do a little directing and work backstage. We provided him, of course, with the stage-hands.

On the day of the rehearsal he arrived at the theatre in a cab, laden down with various pots and pans, bowls and cans. He set the stagehands at different places with these instruments, he became quite excited, and in explaining to each what to beat he became embarrassed. He ran several times from the auditorium up on to the stage and back yet somehow he couldn't get his effect.

The evening of the performance arrived, and Chekhov was all on edge to hear his alarm sound. The strangest noise came forth. It was some kind of cacophony, everyone banged everything in sight and it was impossible to hear the actors.

Next door to the Director's box where Chekhov sat people began to express dissatisfaction with the stage sounds, and then with the play and the author. When Chekhov heard these remarks he sank deeper and deeper into his box and finally he left it altogether and came to sit modestly in my dressing room.

Chekhov liked to come ahead of the performance to sit and watch actors putting on their make-up, to see how their faces are altered by the grease-paint. And whenever he saw a particular line put on transform the face to look like the character in the given part, he would suddenly be overjoyed and laugh out loud with his deep rich voice. Then he would fall silent again and resume his careful watch.

In my opinion Chekhov had a magnificent understanding of physiognomy. Once a close friend of mine came into my dressing room (when Chekhov was there). He was lively, jolly, and thought by society to be rather dissipated. Chekhov observed him closely, his expression was serious and he did not join in the conversation. After the man had gone and all during that evening Chekhov kept asking me all sorts of probing questions about him. When I asked him in return why he was devoting so much attention to him, he said:

"Listen, that man is a suicide."

Such a conclusion seemed ridiculous to me. But I recalled with astonishment his words when, a few years later, I learned that my friend had poisoned himself.

It sometimes happened that I would go to call on Chekhov and have a chat with him. He would be sitting on his sofa, coughing a bit and then throwing his head back so that he could get a better look at me through his glasses. I would be thinking that I was making a jolly impression because when one went to see Chekhov one forgot all about unpleasant things that had happened earlier in the day. Then suddenly, he would seize the opportunity when we were left alone together to ask:

"Listen! You look so strange today. Has anything happened to you?"

Anton Chekhov was offended when anyone called him a pessimist or his characters neurasthenics. Whenever he saw a newspaper in which a critic was making such accusations he would point to the article and say:

"Tell him, tell him (the critic) that he too needs hydrotherapy. . . . He's a neurasthenic too . . . we're all neurasthenics."

Later he might pace up and down his room, coughing and smiling but still showing traces of bitterness by repeating several times and with great emphasis on the letter "i": Pessimist!

Actually Chekhov was the greatest optimist about the future that I ever had the fortune to meet. He painted a cheerful, always lively and confident, beautiful picture of future Russian life. It was only that he looked at the present without falsifying it; he was not afraid of the truth. And the very people who were labelling him a pessimist were the first to look sourly at or fulminate against the present, especially the eighties and the nineties when Chekhov lived. If one remembers his distressing ailment, which caused him so much suffering, his loneliness in Yalta and the fact that despite these he always had a cheerful expression on his face, was always full of interest in everything about him—then one can scarcely find any traits on which to base a portrait of a pessimist.

In the Spring of 1902 the theatre went on tour to St. Petersburg. Chekhov was in Yalta at the time and very anxious to join us but the doctors refused to let him leave. We were playing in the Panayev Theatre and I remember that I rather feared we would not be allowed to put on *The Little People* by Gorki.

We were to give a special advance performance of it for the censor. Among those present on this occasion were Grand Dukes, Ministers, various officials from the Censorship Office and others. They were to decide whether or not we were to be allowed to give the play. We did as delicate a job as we could and we made certain cuts of our own accord.

In the end the play was passed. The censor asked only that one phrase be deleted. ". . . in the house of the merchant Romanov. . . ."

The first performance was given. A dozen armed policemen were concealed about the premises. A lot of seats were occupied by the secret police—in short the theatre was in a state of martial law.

Fortunately there were no incidents. The performance was a huge success.

Olga Knipper fell ill during the second performance. Her illness proved dangerous and called for a serious operation. She was carried out on a stretcher and sent by ambulance to the hospital.

Telegrams flew back and forth between Yalta and St. Petersburg. Chekhov who was ill himself could be told only half the truth. Obviously he was seriously upset and his telegrams, so full of care and concern, show what an extraordinarily gentle, tender person he was. Nevertheless and despite all his efforts he was not allowed to leave Yalta.

The tour was over but Olga Knipper could not be moved. The company dispersed. After a week or two Olga Knipper was taken to Yalta. The operation had not been a success so she fell ill again and took to her bed. The dining room in Chekhov's house was converted into a bedroom for the invalid and Anton Chekhov took care of her as the tenderest of nurses.

Of an evening he would sit in the next room and re-read some of his own short stories which he was collecting for an anthology. Some of them he had quite forgotten and as he read them over he would roar with laughter, because he found them full of both fun and wit.

When I urged him to get on with his new play he would say: "But here it is, here . . ." and with that he would bring out a little bunch of papers covered with his fine handwriting.

Amid all the excitement and anxieties Chekhov still did not give up hope of leaving Yalta and moving to Moscow. Long evenings were spent in describing in detail the personalities and the life of the theatre. He was so interested in Moscow that he asked all the time about what was being built there, and where. He insisted on knowing on what corner what house was being built, in what style, who was building it, how many floors it contained and so on. Then he would smile and sometimes remark:

"Listen! That's just fine!"

He was so delighted with all cultural and building developments. Yet as a doctor Chekhov was probably not very far-sighted because he decided to move his wife to Moscow when she was obviously far from being able to travel.

They came up to Moscow just at the time that we were holding the spring examinations for our [theatre] school. These were held in a special place . . . prepared by S. T. Morosov for rehearsals. The stage was as large as in our theatre but the audience space was small.

On the very day of their arrival Chekhov and his wife hurried over there. The next day Olga Knipper-Chekhov was taken very seriously ill. She was near death, indeed hope of her recovery was abandoned. Chekhov never left her side day or night, he himself prepared compresses for her, etc. We took turns standing watch at his house, not because of the patient who was well cared for and in any case was forbidden all visitors but rather for the sake of keeping up Chekhov's spirits.

On one of the worst days, when the patient's life was dangerously threatened, all Chekhov's close friends gathered and discussed which doctor of their acquaintance should be sent for. As always happens each one stood up for his own doctor. Among those put forward there was one whose name had been quite clouded by some professionally unethical behaviour.

When he heard this name mentioned Chekhov expressed himself in no uncertain terms and said that if they called in this particular doctor he would have to move to America.

"Listen," he said, "I'm a doctor. This would cost me my profession. . . ."

Summer holidays began, everyone left town, but Olga Knipper-Chekhov was no better. She was still in a precarious condition.

Until this time and despite my long acquaintance with Chekhov I still never felt at ease with him. . . . My wife, always felt freer with him than I ever could. I cannot describe what the two of them talked about but their conversation was light and easy and it cheered and amused Chekhov who was himself so natural and simple.

It was really only in these long days when I sat in the room with Chekhov and next door to his desperately ill wife that for the first time I achieved a simple, easy relationship with him. . . .

The topic which loomed largest in our conversation was the new theatre being built for us on Kamergerski Lane. As Chekhov could not leave the house we had the plans and drawings brought to him.

During his wife's illness Chekhov himself grew very thin and weak. . . . Their windows opened onto a narrow street, in June the air was awful, it was dusty and hot and one could not move. Everyone had left town. The only ones who remained were my wife and I and Vishnevski. And even my time was more than up. I was supposed to leave to take a cure which had to be finished before the new season began. So poor Chekhov seemed destined to remain alone, but Vishnevski who was sincerely fond of him, decided to stay on. I went abroad with my family.

The only distraction Chekhov had during this time was an excellent juggler at the "Aquarium," whom he went to watch from time to time when his wife had recovered sufficiently so that he felt he could leave her. Finally, it was almost the end of June, we got word that Olga Knipper-Chekhov was well enough to go out, but there was no possibility of her undertaking the long journey to Yalta. And meantime Chekhov himself was languishing in Moscow.

So we proposed that he and his wife and Vishnevski occupy our wing of the house on my mother's estate where we usually spent our summers. This was near Moscow, on the Yaroslavl railway. The station was called Tarasovka and the Alexeyev estate was known as Lyubimovka. The three of them and a trained nurse soon went down there. But how they spent the summer I know only from hearsay.

(1907)

Messages about The Cherry Orchard

Telegram: October 20, 1903

I have just read the play. Deeply moved, scarcely control myself. Am in unheard-of state of enthusiasm. Consider the play the finest of all the fine things you have written. Cordial congratulations to the genius author. I feel, I treasure every word. Thank you for great pleasure already received and also in store.

Letter: same date

Dear Anton Pavlovich:

According to me your *Cherry Orchard* is your best play. I have fallen in love with it even more deeply than with our dear *Seagull*. It is not a comedy, not a farce, as you wrote—it is a tragedy no matter if you do indicate a way out into a better world in the last act. It makes a tremendous impression, and this by means of half tones, tender water-color tints. There is a poetic and lyric quality to it, very theatrical; all the parts, including that of the vagrant, are brilliant. If I were to choose one of the parts to suit my taste, I would be in a quandary, for every one of them is most alluring. I fear this is all too subtle for the public. It will take time for it to understand all the shadings. Alas, how many stupidities we will have to hear about this play! Nevertheless it will have a tremendous success because as a play it holds you. It is so completely a whole one cannot delete a single word from it. It may be that I am prejudiced, yet I cannot find any defect in this play. Oh yes there is one: it requires too great, too subtle actors to bring out all its charms. We shall not be able to do that. When we had our first reading together I was worried by one thing: I was instantly carried away, and my feelings caught up by the play. This was not the case with *The Seagull* or *The*

Three Sisters. I am accustomed to a rather vague impression from a first reading of your plays. That is why I was afraid that when I read it for the second time it would not capture me again. Nothing of the sort happened. I wept like a woman, I tried to control myself, but could not. I can hear you say: "But please, this is a farce. . . ." No, for the ordinary person this is a tragedy. I sense an attitude of a special kind of tenderness and affection towards this play. I scarcely heard a word of criticism, yet you know how actors love to be critical. Apparently this time they were all instantly won by it. If someone by chance does utter a word of criticism I merely smile and do not bother to argue. I am only sorry for the critic. Someone said: the fourth is the best act, and the second is least successful. I have only to go over the second act scene by scene and that critic is demolished. The fourth act is good just because the second act is magnificent and vice versa. I proclaim this play *hors concours,* and not subject to criticism. Anyone who does not see that is a fool. That is my sincere conviction. I shall act in it with delight. If I could do so I should love to play all the parts, including that of dear Charlotte. Thank you, dear Anton Pavlovich, for the immense pleasure you have already given and for that which is yet to come. How I wish I could give up everything else, shake off the yoke of playing Brutus, and work on nothing but *The Cherry Orchard* all day. This horrible Brutus weighs on me and draws all the juice out of me. I hate him more than ever after (reading) the sweet *Cherry Orchard.*

My warms regards to you and I beg you not to take me for a neurotic lady admirer.

Your affectionate and devoted,
C. Alexeyev (Stanislavski).

Letter: November 2, 1903

I think I have just found the set for the first act. It is a very difficult set. The windows must be close enough to the front of the stage so that the cherry orchard will be seen from the entire auditorium; there are three doors; one would wish to show a bit of Anya's room, bright and virginal. The room is a passage way, but one must be made to feel that here (in the nursery) it is cozy, warm and light; the room has fallen into disuse, there is a slight sense of vacancy about it. Moreover the set must be comfortable and contain a number of planned acting areas. I think we are now able to encompass all this. Do you remember that last year Simov showed you a model which was made for the Turgenyev play, *Where the Thread Is Thin It Breaks*? At the time we decided, with your approval, to save the set for the last act of your play. I have been looking at the model now and find that, with a few alterations, it is very suitable (for the fourth act). If you recall the model, have you any objections? As I write, the third act of *Uncle Vanya* is beginning. There is an enthusiastic response to it, it's the eighty-ninth performance, and we took in 1400 rubles despite the fact that last night we played *The Three Sisters*. So you have earned one hundred and forty rubles today. That's not important. But do you know what is important? It's that this year as never before the audience is really understanding you, they listen in absolute silence. Not a cough in the house despite the bad weather.

Letter: November 19, 1903

. . . I have been busy working on the second act and finally have it in shape. I think it has come out charmingly. Let's hope the scenery will be successful. The little chapel, the ravine, the neglected cemetery in the middle of an oasis of trees in the open steppes. The left side and the centre will not have any wings. You will see only the far horizon. This will be produced by a single semi-circular backdrop with attachments to deepen the perspective. In the distance you see the flash of a stream and the manor house on a slight rise, telegraph poles and a railroad bridge. Do let us have a train go by with a puff of smoke in one of the pauses. That might turn out very well. Before sundown there will be a brief glimpse of the town, and towards the end of the act, a fog: it will be particularly thick above the ditch downstage. The frogs and corncrakes will strike up at the very end of the act. To the left in the foreground a mown field and a small mound of hay, on which the scene is played by the group out walking. This is for the actors, it will help them get into the spirit of their parts. The general tone of the set is like that of a Levitan painting. The landscape is that of the province of Orel not of lower Kursk.

The work is now being carried on as follows: Nemirovich-Danchenko rehearsed the first act yesterday and today I wrote (the plan for) the following acts. I haven't rehearsed my own part yet. I am still undecided about the sets for acts three and four. The model is made and came out well, it is full of mood and besides it is laid out so that all parts of it are visible to all in the auditorium. Down front there is something like shrubbery. Farther upstage are the stairs and billiard room. The windows are painted on the walls. This set is more convenient for the ball. Still a small voice keeps whispering in my ear that if we have one set, which we change in the fourth act, it would be easier and cozier to play in. The weather, alas, is murderous. Everything is melting again and it rains frequently.

Yours,
C. Alexeyev.

Telegram from St. Petersburg: April 2, 1904

Success of *Cherry Orchard* very great, incomparably greater than in Moscow. After third act there were insistent calls for author. The connoisseurs are rapturous over play. Newspapers not very understanding. Company in high spirits. I am triumphant. Congratulations.

Alexeyev.

PART THREE

"My system is the result of lifelong searchings...."

My system is the result of lifelong searchings.... I have groped after a method of work for actors which will enable them to create the image of a character, breathe into it the life of a human spirit and, by natural means, embody it on the stage in a beautiful, artistic form.

(Undated)

When we founded the Moscow Art Theatre we set ourselves not only artistic but also social goals. We knew then and we know even better now that you cannot have great art without great thought and a great public.

(1935)

Like every art the theatre must deepen its consciousness, refine its feelings, raise the level of its culture. When a spectator leaves the theatre he should be able to look at life and his times with deeper perception than when he came into the theatre.

(Undated)

On Reaching the Public

...Only now have we begun to realize that it is not the power of the impression we make on the spectators, but its quality that counts: to make a fleeting effect is not the aim of the theatre. It is much more worthwhile not to have the public make a noise and shout, but to have them undergo a more lasting influence, to have impressions sink deep into their hearts, take root and remain forever a part of their being.

It is infinitely worthwhile when theatrical impressions become living impressions, when the actors in the plays become close, beloved friends. All the great actors of the past, partly consciously and partly unconsciously, sought to arrive at this relationship. And how chagrinned they would be to see how little following generations understood and used the heritage they left!

The changes in what the public demands of the theatre come about very quickly. Nowadays the public is extremely sensitive. It now wants to see real life on the stage, not just an external presentation of it, but its deeper content, real feelings, its genuine logic, real normal movements. To achieve this inner life which you might call "spiritual naturalism" there is one paramount condition: *You must not live on the stage for the purpose of entertaining the spectators, you must live for yourself.*

The less an actor plays for the public the more mysterious and indefinable will be his bond with it, the more intimate and profound.

And I consider our most important achievement to be the fact that the spectators we have won are not just people who have been entertained by us, but thinking and feeling human beings.

129

There is no question but that in these fifteen years our theatre has gone through a great and complicated evolution; we have completed a certain cycle in our searchings....

For we have been searching ever since the very first day of our existence. We were searching for the truth, for fine emotions, we searched for them in a realistic theatre, in a stylized theatre. ...From the external realism which marked our first period we have now come to what might be called "spiritual realism."...

To mark the stages through which we passed, suffice it to name the authors of our plays:

I A. Tolstoy: *Tsar Fyodor Ivanovich:* We approached this play from a purely realistic angle. But this realism was a protest against stale, cliché acting, the misunderstood old "traditions"; it was a reaction against pseudo-romanticism, against acting that had no genuine flesh and blood content, but was all empty craft. The art of the theatre must be the art of experiencing, not merely presenting a part. One can admire this latter but you cannot live on it.... The public is already revolted by cliché actors of this representational type—they want to see real emotions, based on their own living logic....

II A. Chekhov: Chekhov had a decisive part in our evolution. In the beginning, perhaps subconsciously, we were able to portray the "inner flow," the soul of the Chekhov plays that was covered over by the words. For Chekhov characters use certain words, but these do not reveal their life and emotions. Behind these words the "human melody" lies hidden. But now that we act with more subtlety and depth, Chekhov is ever our playwright.

III M. Gorki: He is very close to us because of what he preaches. He revealed to us new paths in acting.

IV H. Ibsen: He attracted us through his philosophy. We sought to reproduce the power of his reason, the power of his logic, which is the fascinating part of Ibsen.

V K. Hamsun: *The Drama of Life:* This was an experiment in stylized theatre. The most important parts of *The Drama of*

Life are the great sweeps, the great volume of inner emotions which we tried to portray by means of stylization.

VI I. Turgenyev: He was very important to us as a writer because of his tremendous inner content. Remember how austerely we set his play, from the point of view of externals, how sparing we were even of our gestures.... And in between Hamsun and Turgenyev I would interpolate Dostoyevski, who offers the actor the opportunity to show elemental qualities, passions, those same "sweeps of emotions" which run through *The Drama of Life.*

VII Molière: In his play *The Imaginary Invalid* we tried to achieve a pattern of inner experience, a kind of "inner musical score." Still it had to be based on a constant close relationship to life.

If we are reproached because of the famous instrument in *The Imaginary Invalid* it is because people do not recognize in that detail the tragedy of life, its genuine truth.... After all, in reply to the King's question Molière answered: "C'est la vie."

This "inner musical score" can be based only on the most spontaneous, naturalistic (*in the sense of naturalness*) feelings....

A director who is putting on a play can be compared to a chemist. He has before him the author and the actor. He finds the real essence of the one and of the other and puts them into some kind of retort. Then he waits. He waits for a long time until a kind of synthesis is produced. So that when people talk of putting on a play with five rehearsals they are talking of a kind of rubber-stamp acting, not of creative acting.

What do we call a six months' baby? We call it a premature baby, not full term. That's what a play is when it is rushed into performance, it's a premature baby too....

But the director in our theatre has also passed through a whole evolution. In the past we directors prepared everything—the sets, scenery, production—and we said to the actor: "Act this way."

Now we prepare everything for the actor, but only after we have ascertained exactly what his needs are and what will appeal to him most of all. . . .

That is what we have come to: we have arrived at "spiritual realism."

—from a talk given on the 15th Anniversary
of the founding of the Art Theatre (1915)

Conversation in an Actor's Dressing Room

Actor: What's wrong? I wept but the audience was cold.

Director: What about the other actors on the stage with you, did they weep?

Actor: I don't recall. I didn't notice.

Director: Are you telling me that you did not sense whether or not your emotions reached them?

Actor: I was so excited. I was watching the audience so closely that I did not notice the other actors. I tell you I was playing at such a pitch that I don't remember anything except myself and the audience!

Director: And what about the reason for your being there on the stage?

Actor: What do you mean—the reason for my being on the stage?

Director: You were there for the purpose of being in some relationship with the characters in the play as designated to you by the author. What other object can an actor have for entering the scene?

Actor: Then what about the audience?

Director: If your feelings are conveyed to the other actors playing with you and if they are affected by them you can rest assured that the audience will be carried away by them and not miss a single shading in your emotional experiences. But if your feelings do not reach even your partner who is standing beside you how do you expect them to reach that absent-minded, restless spectator way off

133

in the twentieth row? Think less about the audience and be more aware of the other characters in the play standing right with you on the stage.

Actor: It would seem to me that an actor plays in the first instance for the audience and not for his fellow actors, whom he has already bored to death during rehearsals. The playwrights entrust us with their works in order to have us convey them to the masses.

Director: Do not belittle our art. Are we to be merely agents, middlemen, between the playwright and the public? No, we are creators in our own right. And does our creativeness consist of no more than reading a role to the public and conversing with it? On the stage we live first of all for ourselves, because we have the ability to desire to live by the emotions of a part and the ability to share them with those who are living on the stage with us. As for the spectator, he is an accidental witness. Speak up so that he can hear you, place yourself in the right parts of the stage so that he can see you, but for the rest, forget entirely about the audience and put your mind solely on the characters in the play. It is not for the actor to be interested in the spectator but the other way around; the spectator should be engrossed in the actor. The best way to be in contact with the audience is to be in close relationship to the characters in the play.

(1933)

On Drama Criticism and Critics

The mutual relations between the actors on the stage and the drama critics are not normal. Their common enterprise rather divides than unites them. Where does the fault lie? It is unfortunate that the drama critics, by virtue of the power of the printed word, have taken up an embattled position vis à vis the theatre; it is unfortunate that they have assumed the role of prosecutor. It is of course as much to be regretted that many actors have picked up the challenge thrown down by their brothers in arms in art.... Unarmed, deprived of all means of fighting back, they either hide their resentment against the press inside themselves, or they ignore it completely.

Thus their collaboration has turned into an enmity, which is bad for our art and for society itself.

This abnormality of relations between the critics and the stage came about because of the evanescence and short life of our art. These peculiar qualities render it impossible to check up on criticism and make the protests of the actors unprovable. Actually what the actor creates on the stage dies the minute he stops creating it. An impression is left but it is intangible and disputed. It is difficult to judge our transient creations by the passing impression of a critic.

Is there any amelioration possible in this morbid inter-relationship?

The fact that criticisms are indefinite and cannot be checked makes it impossible to establish any proper ethical basis for the mutual relations between stage and critics. Criticism will continue to depend on the decency of the critic and the actor in each individual case.

In defense of the critic it must be said that his art requires unusual talent, an emotion memory, knowledge and personal qualities. All this is rarely combined in one person, and that is why good drama critics are extremely rare.

In the first place a drama critic must be a poet and an artist in order to judge at one and the same time the literary accomplishment of the playwright, and the imaginative creative form given to it by the actor.

The critic must be a fine writer. He must have complete control over his pen and his words in order to set down clearly and vividly all the subtlest twists and turns of his feelings and thoughts. He must have an exceptional memory, not that of an accountant, to set down the exact number of curtain calls, the flowers and other gifts offered to the actors, or any other external attributes of success, but that other type, the memory of emotions which brings back past impressions with all their minute details and sensations.

A critic must be sensitive, must possess the imagination to comprehend and magnify the ideas of the playwright and the actors so that he can distinguish between their joint work.

A critic must have a wide knowledge of science and literature, so that when he analyzes the plays of many centuries and different kinds of people he will be able to judge people and their lives as pictured by the playwright and the actors. He must have a probing mind to dissect a creative work.

A critic must be perfectly versed in the technique of writing and the technique of theatre art in all its aspects, beginning with the psychology of creativeness in an actor and ending with the external conditions of his work, the mechanics of stagecraft and the conditions of the theatrical enterprise.

The critic must know and sense the psychology of the audience so that he may find the key to the secret places of their hearts, where the best impulses of the human soul are hidden, and introduce the ideas of the playwright and actors into those secret places.

A critic must be absolutely impartial, a high-minded human being, so that he may inspire confidence in his opinion, and also make noble use of the great power over people the printed word holds. For this same purpose the critic must have experience and self-control.

He should be familiar with the theatre arts of other peoples. He should ... but the list is endless.

Is it to be wondered at that good critics are so rare?

In the great majority of cases a drama critic lacks one or the other of the above assets or capacities—that is why his work is not complete, it is one-sided. Very few understand our special approach to the stage and its technique, or the psychology of those who create images. It is even more rare to come across people who are familiar with the mechanics of the stage, and conditions of work in the theatre.

These deficiencies completely deprive the critic of the capacity to judge what is to be expected of the theatre, what the theatre can or cannot do—there the opinion of such a critic cannot be of value.

(1909)

Why and When Play Melodrama*

To those who think of Stanislavski as having been predominantly interested in introspective, soul-searching plays—such as those by Chekhov, Gorki, Tolstoy, Dostoyevski—it may come as a surprise that he also threw himself with great gusto into lighter plays, commedia dell' arte and even melodrama. His interest in melodrama was twofold: as a legitimate dramatic form of special character requiring the talents of superb actors and as a kind of play in which to train young actors. When Stanislavski was asked about the general impression that melodramas were played only by second-rate actors, he replied*:

"That is not altogether true. A remarkable melodrama is created in its first production; it either comes to life then or it dies and no one remembers its existence. That is why the bringing out of a melodrama is dependent on the participation in it of magnificent actors and on a magnificent production. Opening night tickets are at a high premium. After that other theatres copy the production, actors play the parts by hearsay about the original performers, directors follow the first method used, the production plan, the scenery—everything is meticulously aped.

"Perhaps you have noticed how, in the old printed editions of melodramas, they always give the stage directions and the scheme of movement. That was already introduced by Pixérécourt. I have his copy of one melodrama. It is a director's prompt book complete with the whole production scheme and design for the sets."

In speaking of melodrama as a proving ground for the younger recruits in the theatre, Stanislavski's attitude was: "The basic

---

* All explanatory material added by Editor.

WHY AND WHEN PLAY MELODRAMA

problem in melodrama is to execute to the full and as interestingly as one can all the physical actions outlined by the author.... This obliges an actor to draw on his fantasy, it develops faith in his actions, affords him sincerity of feelings, spontaneity."

For these reasons he greatly encouraged the proposal of two young directors in the Moscow Art Theatre, Gorchakov and Markov, to put on the old Dennery melodrama, laid in the days of the French Revolution, known in America as "The Two Orphans." A film version was produced by Griffith under the title "Orphans of the Storm" and the main roles were played by Lillian Gish and her sister Dorothy. The story is that Griffith was absorbed by the idea of doing a film on the Faust story but Lillian Gish held out for "The Two Orphans" because she knew that it had been played in over forty languages and had never been a failure.

After Stanislavski saw a rehearsal of the first part of the play he made certain comments and offered suggestions. As a steno-graphic record was kept of rehearsals at the Moscow Art Theatre, these remarks can be repeated verbatim. They give a vivid picture of how he worked with his actors.

For readers not familiar with the plot it will suffice to describe the scenes being rehearsed: Henriette and Louise, two pretty orphans, arrive in Paris where they have a distant cousin, a physician, who holds out some hope of curing Louise of her blindness. They were to be met on their arrival by stagecoach from Normandy by an old uncle, Martin. But unfortunately Henriette was seen earlier at a country fair by the wicked Marquis de Prelle who has arranged with Picard, a kind of shady agent, to drug old Martin and abduct Henriette. Louise is left, alone and blind, in the strange city.

Stanislavski took up the work of each actor in detail, chiding the actress who played the kidnapping Mère Frochard for her horror-inspiring make-up by saying: "With a face like that you will never be able to get near enough to a child to steal it. Chil-

dren will run in the opposite direction as soon as you come around
the corner. Mère Frochard has a fascinating, most good-natured
exterior. Everyone thinks she is a saint. No one would ever suspect her of the things she does. It is only when she is at home that
one can see her true face." He commended the actor who played
the hunchback, Pierre, whose kind heart and gift of music enable
the spectator to pierce his unattractive exterior and see the beauty
of his inner world. "I realize why you made yourself so good-
looking. You wanted in advance to appeal to my pity and you
hoped I would say: 'What a shame that such a handsome young
man is a cripple!' But there is another approach. You can show
what is beautiful despite all obstacles. Great actors used to hide
their characters as long as they could from the public, playing at
a kind of hide-and-seek with the plot. Less gifted actors do not
quite trust themselves in such a complex game. The villain is
made up to look repulsive and the long-suffering hero wears a
blond wig." After various other comments Stanislavski suddenly
said:

"And now I want to make sure that all the blinds are closely
drawn and all the doors shut. Put out all lights." Then he rose
from his place in the audience, groped his way to the farther end
of the room where the rehearsal had taken place and, from the
extreme end of it, called to the actress who took the part of
Louise:

"May I ask you to come over here to me?"

"Yes, of course."

A wave of merriment swept over the room but Stanislavski put
an abrupt stop to it:

"I shall ask you to maintain quiet, absolute quiet. The quiet
that enveloped Louise when she was left alone in the square."

Stanislavski spoke in a tone of such absolute command that the
whole room was silent. The actress picked her way in the dark
across the stage. Every piece of furniture, every prop became a
real obstacle. When she stumbled over someone and excused

herself her voice became more and more strained. But no one spoke to her. When she finally reached the place where she expected to find Stanislavski he was not there. She called to him, but the silence was as unbroken as ever. No one knew where he had gone. As Louise wandered through the scenery, lost and alone, she suddenly began to sob and call in a pitiful, tentative, timid voice: "Henriette, where are you?"

Stanislavski by now had returned to his own seat in the audience and there was a great satisfaction in his voice as he said:

"That was magnificent! Now, do you realize what the silence of that Paris square means to Louise when she is left alone, what the darkness means?"

"I understand," replied the actress and her voice trembled.

"Turn up the lights," ordered Stanislavski. "Now you know what blindness is. You became frightened because we were all silent. That is how silent Paris is all around Louise. Perhaps such things have happened to her before. As a general rule people instinctively avoid a blind person, when they catch a sight of one coming they step out of his way. This is a kind of atavism, brutal egoism, fear that a blind person will require some service one cannot refuse. Louise knows that the strange city remains silent although people may be passing by, others may be watching her from the windows. If that is possible it should be arranged for, it emphasizes the emptiness of the square. This emptiness is not in the landscape, not in the scenery ... but in the egoism of the people in a large city—that is what grips one and must grip the audience. This conveys the tragic position of Louise, it underscores the fact that her good angel Henriette has left her. It was very good that you found the right word to say just now, the name of your sister, because it means that the exercise took on the reality of the subject of the play. That is the goal of every exercise.

"Now fix in your mind the physical and psychological pattern of the exercise:

1. It came to you as a surprise. In parallel fashion the situation into which Louise is thrust also comes as a surprise to her. There is no need here for any inner preparatory work.

2. You could not find your way, you bumped into things and people, you excused yourself, your eyes were *open*. You walked and walked but *you were not acting*. You really searched for me, you were not just playing a blind girl.

3. You were *embarrassed* to call for help. Your voice took on a peculiar tone, half a cry. You uttered abrupt exclamations.

4. You became frightened *because you did not know what would happen next*.

"All this taken together adds up to blindness. It must be understood as an inner sense of a person, not merely an external defect. Every so-called external characteristic of a part has its psychological inner counterpart, a reflection of, reaction to surrounding realities. Little is said or written about this; people who have physical defects do not like to be reminded of them. But an actor must know about them.... However, what the spectator must have is the *primary impact* of blindness, the first ten minutes of blindness for someone, not all the commentary, all the literature on the subject. The actor should be able to convey all physical defects of his role by means of inner sensation."

Next Stanislavski passed to the analysis of the role of Picard, the agent hired by the Marquis de Prelle to get rid of old Uncle Martin before the two orphan girls arrive from Normandy. After some discussion he proposed to play the part of Martin in the scene in front of a tavern. What follows is the transcript of the rehearsal:

Picard: (approaching the table at which old Martin is seated) Well, old man, waiting for someone?

Martin: Yes.... Maybe.... I am.

Picard: Didn't come, did they?

Martin: What makes you think I am waiting for the stagecoach from Normandy? (his tone full of suspicion)

Picard: I ... er ... well, people around here are usually waiting for the stagecoach to arrive. I'm waiting too (the actor improvised these words and then went back to the text of the play). Perhaps we can have a couple of drinks together?

Martin: (with unexpected eagerness) I don't mind if I do.

Picard: Here there, mine host, bring us two mugs of your best cider! (to Martin) Who are you waiting for? Your old woman I'll be bound. (he draws what is obviously a soporific powder unobtrusively from his pocket)

Martin: (withdrawing slightly, his tone full of suspicion) Yes, yes, my old woman, my old woman and perhaps someone else too.

The host brings the mugs of cider and the actor playing Picard waits until, according to the usual plan for acting the scene, old Martin will lean down and buckle his shoe. But Stanislavski in the part does not lean down and afford Picard the opportunity to slip the powder in his drink. After an enforced pause Picard goes on talking.

Picard: Here's to you!

Martin: Thanks. Thanks. Ah, how I wish I were a little younger ... a little stronger....

The young actor is embarrassed at the turn of the conversation, holds the powder in his hand, keeps the conversation going.

Picard: Why do you wish you were stronger? You can go anywhere you want to....

Martin: No, no. I'm not what I used to be ... not anymore. ... Now I want to sleep ... get to bed early too—that's old age creeping up on me. Yet I can't sleep! I can't get to sleep! (Stanislavski said the lines with such a beady bright expression it was perfectly obvious he had no idea of dozing off according to the directions given in the text of the play.)

The young actor playing the part of Picard then announced

that there were no more words for him to say and that the scene between them was over. Stanislavski remonstrated with him and expressed the conviction that if an agent of the type of Picard had found that he could not drug his victim he would surely have had some other way of getting rid of him. The young actor insisted that the stage directions said: "he makes him fall asleep by putting a powder in his drink...."

"That was put there for the first production from which the printed text was drawn. Obviously the two actors who played this scene did it remarkably well," said Stanislavski, and added: "If all you are interested in is carrying out a piece of stage business from a printed page your acting will never be anything but a stencil copy. The author says only to put him to sleep. In every theatre these two actors will accomplish this in their own way. The tradition of melodrama is to give the fullest freedom of physical action to the actor provided he does not do anything which is mere patent trickery. All he is required to do is to keep within the logic of the plot and its line of action. Let's play the scene over again."

This time the young actor had the idea of chasing an imaginary fly off old Martin's mug of cider and incidentally dropping the powder in it. But Stanislavski in a surprise gesture knocked the mug off the table. This was too much.

"But, Mr. Stanislavski, we'll never get anywhere if old Martin doesn't take his drink!"

"If that is what you think, your imagination is not working very actively. In the stage directions it says you are to put Martin to sleep, but how you do it is not indicated. Therefore old Martin is fully within his rights to drink or not to drink. And Picard must be prepared to get the old man out of the way with any number of stratagems."

As a spur to the invention of the actors Stanislavski asked Mikhailov, one of the older members of the theatre, to play the scene with him impromptu. Stanislavski instantly converted himself into the jaunty self-assured Picard and Mikhailov was transformed into a suspicious, kindly old Martin. From the start they ad libbed freely.

Stanislavski: Fine evening.

Mikhailov: It is, rather....

Stanislavski: (taking out a pretended snuff box with a gesture that made the audience realize it was full of dope) Care for a pinch?

Mikhailov: No, thanks.

Stanislavski: (pocketing the snuff box after taking a pinch) Perhaps you'd like a smoke?

Mikhailov: No, I never smoke.

Stanislavski (aside) Curse the old fool. I'll have to offer him a drink. (aloud) Let's have some cider. I'll stand you to a mug.

Mikhailov: Well, perhaps ... but really ... I'm embarrassed....

Stanislavski: Ho there, innkeeper, a couple of mugs of cider! Are you waiting for someone?

Mikhailov: Yes and no, not anyone special. Maybe my nieces will turn up.

In throwing down some coin to pay for the drinks Stanislavski let them casually roll off the table onto the ground. Naturally all three leaned under the table to retrieve the money. Suddenly Stanislavski's hand was seen to reach up from under the table and apparently drop the powder in one of the mugs. But Mikhailov did not let the scene end there. With an expression of suspicion he screwed up his face and looked first into one mug and then the other.

Mikhailov: Would you please exchange mugs with me?

Stanislavski: (quite taken aback by the request as Picard would have been) But why?

Mikhailov: Just so ... please do it.

Stanislavski: Well, if you like.

After examining the two mugs carefully, Mikhailov pushed his mug across the table.

Mikhailov: Mine had more in it than yours, but since you're inviting me to drink you must have that mug. That's the custom!

Stanislavski: I never heard of such a custom.

Mikhailov: Anyway I beg you to take it otherwise I shan't touch a drop.

Stanislavski: (aside) Curse the old man! He wants me to poison myself. (aloud) Thanks. Here's to your health.

But just as he raised the mug to drink from it he was seized with a fit of violent sneezing.

Mikhailov: (sympathetically) Did you catch cold?

Stanislavski: (pretending to take a vial out of his pocket and to pour some of the contents into his handkerchief) Yes, but I have a good remedy for it. (still sneezing he puts the vial on the table)

Mikhailov: What a pretty little bottle. May I look at it?

Stanislavski: (still sneezing) Of course, please do. But you'll have to excuse me for a moment. (Still sneezing he left the table, stepped behind Mikhailov just as he was picking up the vial and slipped the doped handkerchief over his mouth. He made a sign to the tavernkeeper to come.)

Mikhailov: (realizing the game is up) I don't want to sleep... I mustn't go to sleep....

Stanislavski (to the tavernkeeper) Carry him into a back room.

After the scene between the two veteran actors was over the objection was raised to the effect that two really good actors could thus spin any part of the play out indefinitely, to which Stanislavski replied:

"I don't think that would happen. It takes a long time in rehearsal to work those things out but in actual performance of melodrama the tempo is always headlong and the dialogue very rapid. The director chooses only the best from all such exercises based on the physical action of the play and throws away the rest. But unless these scenes are worked out in detail there is no melodrama. In plays by Ibsen or those based on Dostoyevski you cannot ad lib that way, nor have you any need to do so.

"In general I should like you to understand the kind of atmosphere that must surround the preparation of a melodrama as a dramatic genre and the ardent mood which should take possession of the actors who play in one.

"For one thing there can be no indifference in the hall on the day a melodrama is performed. On that occasion everything must be unusual and unexpected. The audience must be galvanized in advance, there must be sufficient electricity in the air so that everything explodes and true creativeness and inspiration sweep across the stage. This is one more approach to the actor's creative state. Melodrama is drawn from the life of the people, but it is highly concentrated, stripped of extra details and pauses. The only pauses are those allowed to the stars, to let them shoot off some rockets of stunt acting, and there is usually a fixed number of them. When the spectator sees a melodrama he thinks that everything shown in the play must have happened in *real* life. That is why theatrical clichés must be rigourously avoided. Moreover, if a spectator believes that all this happened, as it were, right around him in everyday life, he is extraordinarily moved by it, it makes him weep, it makes him laugh—for laughter is also an indication that a person has been moved if it is the result produced by a character or a situation on the stage and not merely by a tongue stuck out at the public for no good reason.

"Melodrama has always emerged when the populace has been in the throes of high and noble emotions, when there is a sense that these feelings must be expressed, a desire to see them on the stage.... When you have found the right tone for this play... everything will begin to move with increasing speed. It always goes beautifully if it is well prepared. The only thing to arrange most carefully is the end of the performance. The audience never forgives you if you do not give a proper finish, a good final period. That is the part of the great art of a director—the endings of acts and the final curtain." (1927)

147

Young Actors in Mob Scenes

You have just played the finale of the prison scene, the so-called "Storming of the Bastille." This is a mob scene that lasts three minutes and constitutes the culminating point in the play. It represents the summing up in the struggle to have truth and justice prevail, the struggle to free the people from the oppression of a monarchy and the despotic aristocracy that ruled France along with the king. This scene is the triumph of the French Revolution. And what do I see from where I sit in the auditorium? I am ashamed to tell you: I saw the bored, indifferent faces of actors mechanically moving through their stage business!

I have watched you in this finale for several days now. I thought at first that this was something accidental, that you were tired from the pressure of these full-dress rehearsals. Yesterday I even rearranged the schedule in order to give the actors a respite. Yesterday we discussed only motivation. Unfortunately, a few minutes ago, I witnessed the same picture over again: bored faces, cold voices, limp movements. Where is the inspiration, the joy of freedom regained, the mad rhythm which the partisans at the fall of the Bastille poured into the famous *carmagnole*—a national folk dance that was born right there on the square with the smoking ruins of the Bastille as a background? Where is that impulse which inspired the people who stormed the Bastille to carry away stone by stone that dark fortress, symbol of the monarchy?

You are well aware of this fact. You know the rhythm and the tune of the *carmagnole*. But as I saw you just now you would, in my opinion, be incapable of dancing even a vapid polka, let alone a dance full of inner fire and fervid temperament. You would be incapable of heaving a simple brick, let alone the huge stones from the bastions of the Bastille!

I shall have to speak certain bitter truths to you. When you come to me and beg to be taken into our theatre you swear by all that is holy to you that the theatre is for you the great goal of your life, that if you are not permitted to work in the theatre it will mean death to your soul, that you will cease to exist. You assert that you are prepared to do any work you are called on to do in the theatre. The most frequent expression you use is—we are ready to scrub the floors!

Yet if we meet with your wishes, what happens? Scarcely two or three years go by and we see tired, bored, disillusioned faces— and not from scrubbing floors, mind you, but from working creatively on the stage. This is horrible! This is indescribable! This spells death to all our art! The one thing which can destroy the theatre utterly is boredom, boredom flowing from the stage into the auditorium, boredom and the indifference of actors *supposedly* moving, *supposedly* acting, *supposedly* creating something on the stage. This is not worthy of the name of acting. This sets the theatre back fifty years when instead of any sense of the ensemble, of the over-riding common purpose and objective of the spiritual responsibility of the actor for his right to be on the stage, instead of that there was only the theatre of empty show and entertainment.

In your meetings you debate in hot words the new significance of art in Russia, you swear you are devoted to the people and the Revolution, yet when you have the opportunity to put your words and promises into action on the stage, in a profession you yourselves chose, when you are faced with impersonating a people (it is the French people, but that makes no difference), a people with all its many facets—you are bored, you execute with indifference the assignment given you by [the subject of] the playwright and the stage plan of your director. This is a crime. It is a crime committed against yourselves as actors and artists, against the theatre in which you work, against the government which has afforded you the opportunity to live and create in the field of art.

Verbally you enthuse over the Moscow Art Theatre and my system of acting, but in what you do you discredit both the theatre and me. I have tried all my life to found a method on the basis of which the truths of life can be metamorphosed into stage images. This is an objective of immense difficulty. The road towards this goal is not easy but you have already set your feet on it and you have here one possibility to progress along it. This is a modest beginning but it is a very real one: participation in crowd scenes.

Before you lies the marvellous opportunity to metamorphose yourselves—this is the most inspiring, creative process in an actor's mastery of his art. Today some of you represent the revolutionary people of France and others their enemies: the counts, dukes and marquesses and their sycophants. Tomorrow you will play "elected ones" of the Russian people in *Tsar Fyodor,* also their enemies—the boyars, the princes, the feudal lords. The day after tomorrow you will be representatives of Moscow society of the twenties of the last century at the ball at Famusov's (*Sorrow From Wit,* by Griboyedov). What a marvellous opportunity for metamorphosis! Each day a new image, with its actual existence based on history, each one that of a thinking, acting person with his own individual biography, his objective in life and on the stage, his own line of action through to those objectives. Do you think that I am spending my time teaching you that to play a new role all you have to do is to change your costume, your beard, and today handle axes and rifles, tomorrow a shepherd's crook and wear a cap, and the day after that use a lorgnette, cane and fan?

That would be the profanation of everything for the sake of which Nemirovich-Danchenko and I founded the Moscow Art Theatre. That would be its ruin. The glory of the Art Theatre was spread not only by Kachalov, Moskvin, Leonidov, Madame Savitskaya and Olga Knipper-Chekhov,—but also and equally by our crowd scenes. The principles on which we trained our company live and flourish in them—they serve to effect a complete, profound, active revelation in physical and theatrical terms of the ideas and subject of the playwright.

The pride of the Art Theatre has always been the mob scene "on the Yausa" in *Tsar Fyodor,* the scene in the Forum in *Julius Caesar,* the scene of the mutiny in *Children of the Sun,* the scene-interlude of the guests in *Sorrow From Wit,* the scene in Mokroye in *The Brothers Karamazov,* the scene with the gypsies in *The Living Corpse* and the folk scene in *Pugachovshchina.*

And you with your indifference to crowd scenes, with your bored faces and limp rhythms, wish to rob us of all that we, the elders of the theatre, have stored up over these twenty-five years!

You shall not do it! If you did I would demand that the theatre be closed down and I am convinced that I would be understood by those on whom the authority to do so rests.

Do remember this: the theatre is a collective enterprise in art, a performance in an ensemble in which no single actor, even playing a leading part and playing it with however remarkable skill, can save the situation if he is surrounded by vapidity, boredom, colourlessness at the culminating moment of action in the play.

I will not tolerate undisciplined, "half-baked" conduct on the stage. I do not wish to see, and indeed I have no right to see, bored physiognomies on the stage. I do not have at my disposal any directional devices, tricks of the trade, by which I could cover up one bored face in a crowd scene. One face can spoil a whole scene, spoil it for all the others who may be doing their parts properly, because by the law of contrasts that one face will stand out from the others and attract the attention of the audience. It cannot be hidden, it cannot be masked by anything. It is simpler, better, and more just to take it off the stage, and to suggest to the actor that he go elsewhere to perform.

Let anyone who finds it difficult to take part in crowd scenes come to me and frankly tell me so. I cannot be party to depriving the Art Theatre of its principal glory, its ability to infuse vivid, true life into its crowd scenes, I have no right to do this vis à vis the people who entrusted Nemirovich-Danchenko and me with the management of this theatre. So I shall neither curtail nor cut the crowd scenes as they do in many other theatres, so do not expect this of me.

On the contrary I shall be ruthless in my demands concerning them. All the more so because shortly we shall be opening *The Armoured Train,* a play in which the principal part is played by the people, the Russian people....

Forgive my severity but I am deeply disturbed.

(1927)

What Is the Grotesque?

You say that in the twentieth century Pushkin must be played quite differently, more fully, the very way he wrote, otherwise the images he created tend to become shallow to the point of turning into simple, national types of historic figures. And therefore Pushkin can be presented only in tragic grotesque, as Molière can be in tragicomic grotesque. You, like other innovators, choose to call this highest form of our art—toward which, believe me, I have striven all my life—these supreme artistic creations, by the name of grotesque. To this I reply: "Let them be so called!" Does it matter? Is the point in their denomination? But now we shall examine the grotesque only from this point of view. Now I shall ask you, did you ever in your life see this kind of grotesque? I saw one example of it, it was not ideally perfect, but it was the best that a human man can produce. It was the Othello of Salvini. And I also saw a comic grotesque, or, to be more exact, actors capable of creating it. These were old Zhivokini and Varlamov, both dead now. All they had to do was appear on the stage and say: "How are you?" At that moment they often personified comedy completely. This was not Varlamov coming on to the stage, and perhaps it was not even the incarnation of the good humour of the Russian people in general, but these were seconds and minutes when we saw the embodiment of universal good humour. Who can deny that that was grotesque? I endorse such a statement without the slightest hesitation. But I am puzzled when you begin to tell me that such a super-conscious, supremely perfect creation of a genuine artist, the thing you choose to call grotesque, can be achieved by your students, who are completely untried, who do not have any notion how to speak so that one can sense the inner significance of a phrase or word which rises from the depths to express universal thought and feeling, your students, who are still incapable of feeling what is inside them, who have only achieved a certain external ease through their lessons of dance and plastic movement—they are adorable "puppies," their eyes are not even open yet and they are prattling about the grotesque....

No, this is a delusion! You have simply collected some guinea pigs for research purposes, you are making experiments with them by using your own intuition, experiments not based on practice or knowledge, the experiments of a talented person, the results of which will come as accidentally as they will also vanish. You are not making the effort, so necessary to the grotesque, of finding an approach to the super-conscious (where the grotesque lies hidden) through conscious means.

It is easy enough to call a thing grotesque, but has it really degenerated, become so oversimplified and banal, been degraded to the point of becoming nothing more than external exaggeration without inner justification?

No, genuine grotesque is a vivid and bold externalization based on such tremendous, all-embracing inner content that reach the limits of exaggeration. An actor must not only feel and experience human passions in all their universal, component elements—he must over and above this condense them and produce a manifestation of them so vivid, so irresistible in its expressiveness, so audacious, so bold that it borders on the burlesque. The grotesque may not be unintelligible, there can be no question mark placed after it. The grotesque must be definite and clear to the point of brazenness. It would be too bad if any spectator, after seeing your grotesque, should ask: "Tell me please, what is the meaning of those two crooked eyebrows and the black triangle on the cheek of Pushkin's Miser Knight or Salieri?" It would be too bad if after that you had to explain: "Well, you see the artist wanted to picture a sharp eye. And since symmetry is soothing he introduced that slant...." There lies the grave of the grotesque. It dies and in its place is born a simple riddle, as silly and naïve as the ones they publish in the illustrated magazines for their readers. What do I care how many eyebrows or noses an actor has? Let him have four eyebrows, two noses, a dozen eyes. But they must be justified by the fact that the actor's inner content is so great that two eyebrows, one nose, and two eyes are not enough for him to project all this immense spiritual content. But if the four eyebrows are not based on necessity, if they have no justifiable basis, such grotesque makes the actor smaller, it does not inflate his little being. To inflate something which is nonexistent, to inflate emptiness—that makes me think of blowing soap bubbles. When the form is greater and more powerful than the actual being this latter is bound to be crushed and unnoticed in the tremendous space.... This is the same as putting an infant into the uniform of a seven foot grenadier. However, if the essential being is greater than the form, then that is grotesque....

Yet is it worthwhile breaking our hearts about something which, alas, practically does not exist, something which we see only in the rarest exceptional instances in our art? To tell the truth, have you ever seen a stage creation of such all-embracing content that imperatively called for the enlarged and exaggerated form of the grotesque in which to be expressed? It makes no difference where: in drama, comedy or farce? On the contrary how often one does see a great blown-up form, inflated like a soap bubble, to the point of external, make-believe grotesque, but completely lacking in all content. You must realize that that is just a pie with nothing inside, a bottle without wine, a body without a soul....

Such grotesque without spiritual motive or content...is mere affectation. Alas, alas! Where is the actor who dares to push out to the limits of the grotesque? (No one is forbidden to dream about it.) The fact that some futurist painter put four eyebrows on the actor does not bestow the grotesque on him. No one will interfere with the painter who wants to draw four eyebrows on a piece of paper. But paint them on us? For that he must first gain our permission. Let it be the actor who says: "I am ready. Splash on a dozen eyebrows!" But that I should let the painter put four eyebrows on me for the sake of his winning some laurels? No! I protest! Let him not smear our faces. Can't he find someone else for that? I do not doubt for a minute that a great painter who puts several eyebrows on a face is doing it with a reason. He has reached this point after passing through great suffering, through the torments of disillusion with his previous achievements, which have ceased to satisfy his fantasy and demands, which constantly move ahead. But can we say that the art of our theatre has already gone so far that it can keep pace with the painters of extreme tendencies? When did we ever take the first steps already made by the art of painting? We have not as yet even reached true realism and achieved a standing on a level with the avant garde artists of thirty or more years ago....

—from "Last Talk" with Vakhtangov, the actor and director (1922)

The Inner Pattern of the Role

The personality of a human being is the synthesis of his soul and his outward appearence. The external image of a character portrayed by an actor is very important, yet his soul is of even greater importance. It is easy to interest the public in external appearance because it is material, visible. After having attracted the attention through the external the actor should make use of this attention to show his soul. This is far more difficult.

You can scrutinize a person's soul through his eyes because they are its best expression.

To show one's eyes and their expression to an audience of a thousand people is far from easy. In order to do it one has to direct the attention of the public to one's eyes, the expression of which illuminates the text and gives meaning, significance to it. Obviously to centre their attention across a great space on such a small point as eyes, the large audience must be able to see and study them. For this, one needs to be motionless, and to have time. Thus, in order to show one's eyes one must not distract attention from them by any kind of movement or gestures, and one must choose a location where the eyes and their expression are visible to the public. To accomplish this one's acting must be inspired, otherwise the expression of the eyes will not be interesting, it will have nothing to show, also it must be controlled, calm, to give the public the opportunity really to look at the actor's eyes.

Thus the actor's technique (aside from the question of his personal feelings in his part) consists of (a) catching the attention of the public by his external appearance, (b) being able to hold their attention on his words and gestures, and (c) carrying imperceptibly that attention over to his eyes and then expressing to the public the state of his soul. In order to catch attention by his external appearance this must be artistically truthful, expressive, related to the spiritual mood of the character played.

Gestures should further outline the image of the character and the text to express his spiritual state.

Through the words and the thought inherent in them the public is drawn closer to the soul of the character portrayed.

When an actor comes alive in the image he has created, his feelings will be reflected in his eyes. If he can then show them to the large audience they will read his emotions in them and will join with him in those emotions and thoughts of his character. It is evident that an actor's emotions must be powerful and expressive means, and vivid, too, if they are to arouse a crowd of thousands. . . .

—Remarks during a rehearsal
of Chirikov's *Ivan Mironych* (1904)

The Mysterious World of *The Blue Bird*

. . . We are to stage a dream, a fancy, an intimation, a fairy tale. [*The Blue Bird*] is a fabric of lace. And our tools, those available to the theatrical technique of our day, are coarse and rough. That presents a great technical difficulty.

I shall try to take a few steps along the path of what we are to search for. These steps will be uncertain and perhaps mistaken, for I have read the play through only twice and, of course, I was not able to glimpse all the delicate threads out of which, like those of a spider web, the great poet wove his creation. . . .

Man is surrounded by the mysterious, terrifying, magnificent, incomprehensible. . . . This mysteriousness, or unintelligibility, bears down most heavily on the young, the vital, those who are most aquiver with life on this earth, or it scatters snow on the heads of the helpless blind, or it astounds and dazzles us with its beauties.

We are drawn to the mysterious, we have intimations of it, but we do not understand it.

Sometimes, in moments of exaltation, for an instant our eyes are opened—then the foul air of reality blurs the scarcely-glimpsed, mysterious outline.

In his animal nature man is coarse, cruel and arrogant. He kills his own kind, he eats animal flesh, he destroys nature and believes that everything around him was created for his capricious use. He rules the earth and thinks that he has understood the mysteries of the world. Actually he understands precious little.

The principal things are hidden from man. People live amid material blessings, are further and further removed from spiritual, contemplative life.

Only a few chosen ones possess as their own this spiritual joy. They listen closely to the tiny rustle made by the growth of a blade of grass, or they strain their eyes to glimpse the transparent outlines of worlds we do not know.

Having seen and heard these mysteries of the world, they tell others about them, but these human beings merely stare at any such genius, they smile doubtfully, or even blink their eyes. Thus the centuries roll by, the roar of the cities and towns drowns out the tiny rustle made by the growth of a blade of grass.

The smoke from factories veils the beauty of the world from us; the abundance of manufactured luxury blinds us, and plaster ceilings keep from us the stars and the sky.

We are suffocated, we seek for happiness in the foul air and soot of the life we have made. Occasionally we snatch a bit of real happiness . . . way off, from an open field, bathed in sunshine, but that happiness, like the blue bird, turns black as soon as we enter the shadow of the murky city.

Children are nearer to nature from which they so recently came. They love to meditate. They are capable of love for a toy, they weep when parted from it. Children can enter into the lives of ants, a birch tree, a dog or a cat. To children high joys and pure dreams are accessible.

That is why Maeterlinck surrounded himself with children in *The Blue Bird* and went off with them on a journey through mysterious worlds. He succeeded completely in reproducing the world of child fantasies, fears and dreams. Let us try to throw aside thirty years of our lives and return to our childhood.

The production of *The Blue Bird* must be done with the purity of fancy of a ten-year-old child. It must be naïve, simple, light, full of the joy of living, gay, transparent, like a child's dream; beautiful like a child's fancy, yet together with all that, it must have the grandeur of the idea of a poetic genius and thinker.

May our *Blue Bird* delight the grandchildren and also arouse serious thoughts and deep feelings in the grandmothers and grandfathers.

May the grandchildren, when they return to their homes, experience a joy in being alive, as do Tyltyl and Mytyl in the last act of the play. . . .

May the old people scrape away from their souls the scum that has formed on them, and let them, perhaps for the first time in their lives, look attentively into the eyes of a dog, pat its head gently in token of gratitude for its devotion to man. And there, perhaps, in the quiet of a sleeping city, they may sense in their souls the existence of that faraway Land of Memory, where they will soon be dreaming as they wait for the visit of guests from the earth. . . .

From a speech to The Moscow Art Theatre Company (1907)

On Playing Othello

In 1930, Stanislavski was forced by serious illness to withdraw from a production of *Othello*. To L. M. Leonidov, who was playing the title role, he wrote the following letters while convalescing in Nice.*

... Let us examine the state of feeling in which Othello finds himself. He was unbelievably happy with Desdemona. This was his honeymoon, a dream, the very height of passion. It is this very height of passion which is not conveyed in the way the part is usually played, and indeed the author himself did not emphasize it or give much space to it; yet it is important when it comes to showing what Othello is losing, what he is bidding farewell to in the scene in which you feel you are not successful.

In itself this scene lies on a dividing line. From this point forward Othello plunges downward. Is it possible to bid farewell all at once to a bliss which he has experienced, with which he has lived? Is it easy for him to admit his loss? When a person has torn from him part of the fabric of his life, he is at first stunned, he loses his equilibrium, and then he painfully begins to search for it. First he had his bliss, now how can he go on living without it? In his tortures, in his sleepless nights, a man who is going through a crisis carefully examines his whole life. He weeps for what he has lost; he appreciates it more than ever and at the same time he compares it with his future, with what awaits him, that which his imagination pictures to him.

What does a man need who is performing this great inner work? He needs to withdraw inside himself, to look over his past

* Editor's Note.

and consider his future. This is a moment of profound self-immersion. It is not surprising therefore that a man in this state does not notice what is going on around him, that he is absent-minded, somewhat strange, and that when he comes back from the world of his own thoughts to reality, he is even more horrified and upset than ever, and seeks some pretext for pouring out the bitterness and pain accumulated in the time of his self-immersion. To me then, that is, more or less, Othello's state in this scene. That too was the point of departure of the stage design. That is why Othello rushes to the top of the tower, as he does in this scene, and then dashes down to a sort of subterranean place where weapons of all sorts and other gear are stored, and hides himself from people so that they may not see the condition he is in.

Therefore the line of this scene, according to me, would be drawn more or less in this fashion: He climbs to the tower to express what he feels when he says: "Ha! ha! false to me?" I do not at all agree to the interjection here of: "Ha! ha!" because there is something of a threat in that word and there is no threat in Othello's state here. That is why, when I played it, I changed it, if I am not mistaken, to: "What! False to me, to me . . ." with the emphatic repetition of "me." What does this mean? It means that given the love that had been, given the fact that I gave myself wholly to her, that I am ready to make any sacrifices, she might have said just the words "I love Cassio," and I would have done anything to further her desires: I would have gone away, or I would have stayed near her, to protect her. But how could she furtively betray such devotion, such complete self-immolation, and do it with such diabolical trickery and slyness? This is a devil who has assumed the form of an angel.

I maintain that Othello is not a jealous man. The petty jealousy usually attributed to Othello really applies to Iago. It would appear, as I reason it, that Iago is really jealous, in a shallow, cheap way, of Emilia. Othello is a man of exceptionally noble nature. He cannot bear to live in a world where he is aware that people are so unjust to one another, where they gratuitously scoff at and defile the high-minded love he harbours in himself. And this in the shape of such an ideally beautiful woman, a goddess-like creature of heavenly purity and incorruptibility, of unearthly goodness and tenderness. And all these qualities are so artfully imitated that they cannot be distinguished from the genuine!

To come back to the scene in question: I assert that it is not jealousy but morbid disillusion in an ideal woman, a human being such as the earth has never seen before. This is the deepest pain, the most intolerable suffering. Othello sits for hours without changing his position, with his eyes fixed on a single spot, with his whole being withdrawn inside himself in order to understand and be able to believe in this fiendish deceit. Therefore, when Iago cautiously, like a serpent, emerges unnoticed and speaks, like a doctor to a patient, and says, with unwonted tenderness: "Why, how now, General? No more of that!" Othello shudders in anticipation of the pain that this torturer may cause him. When a doctor arrives with a large instrument to probe a painful wound the patient will groan with the consciousness of the suffering to come. Usually the actors who play Othello have him fall into a rage at this point. Actually he is in a state of most horrible pain. He suffers so much that his former false dream, his illusion of happiness, seems to him at this moment to be real happiness. He sets his illusion of happiness up in contrast to what has now happened and he begins to take leave of life. In all his world he has had only two passions: Desdemona and his military art; as with a great artist his life is divided between a beloved woman and his art.

Thus "O, now for ever, farewell the tranquil mind! Farewell content!" is an adieu, a plaint, a mourning over his second love and not at all a scene of emotional exaltation of military life as it is usually played. I shall applaud you most warmly if you stand motionless, not noticing anything around you, and seeing with your inner eye that whole picture of what is infinitely dear to any real artist in military performance. Stand still, wipe away the tears that course down your cheeks, hold in your sobs, and speak with a barely audible voice as one does in relating something that is of utmost import and sacredness.

Perhaps this soliloquy will be broken by long pauses during which Othello will stand there in a sort of trance, and be silent as he reviews to the end the picture of what he is losing. During other pauses he may, perhaps, bend over the great stone and sob noiselessly, then shudder and somehow shake his head as if he were saying farewell. This is not the emotion of military exultation. It is a mournful farewell before death. After he has bludgeoned his own soul with this farewell he now feels that he must vent his tortures on someone else. He takes out his suffering on Iago. After he has clutched him and very nearly thrown him from the top of the tower, he is aghast at what he might have done; he retreats to the large space by the flat stone and throws himself down on it trembling and racked with noiseless sobs. Then he sits up straight, like a child, in a child-like poise, on the stone, and asks forgiveness and pours out his grief to Iago who stands below him. At the end of the scene, when it has grown almost dark, the moon is coming up and the stars have begun to shine, Othello, standing on the high platform calls to Iago to come up to him; and up there, between the sky and the sea, he, a man wounded in his best feelings, calls to witness the moon appearing on the horizon as he performs the terrible rite: he pronounces his vow of revenge. . . .

(10 February 1930)

. . . . Here is the reply to your two objections:
. . . . When you reach Cyprus your desire is to rush at once to Desdemona. I advised you to receive the deputation first and then let yourself go and play the scene of your meeting with Desdemona.

You and I are seeking the same thing, which is to push your

scene with Desdemona out into the foreground. It was in order to achieve this that I reasoned the way I did. To dash in, embrace her and play a passionate scene—that is what everyone does. That is what everyone in the audience expects. Therefore there is nothing unexpected in your entrance and unless you can achieve that, you have no edge.

But there is another drawback: How can you play the scene of receiving the deputation after the tender meeting with Desdemona? This meeting calls for great intimacy; afterwards you must go home and to bed. But if I see the actor cool off and take up his duties as governor general, things would look bad from the point of view of love-making. I, as a spectator, would cease to speculate about what might be going on after the end of the scene, during the intermission, when love-making should be at its most ardent.

It seemed to me when I planned this scene that it would be more vivid, powerful and advantageous from the angle of the lovers if Othello first discharged his gubernatorial duties, during which he would be constantly excited and looking around as unobtrusively as possible for a glimpse of Desdemona. Then, having done with the formalities, there would be the intimate scene and exit.

I think that would better achieve what both you and I want. It is impossible to tell without trying it out.

As to your other objection: You are against the mutiny on the island and explain why you are right. Things can be explained that way. But now let us ask Shakespeare: what does he want of Iago? Look at Iago's words: ". . . am I to put our Cassio in some action that may offend the isle. . . ." Then to put down the mutiny Cassio must be removed from his office.

This is so crystal clear and supports my comments to such an extent that no further explanations are needed.

Of course, the director of the play can carry Iago's plan out to its conclusion or cut it off at an earlier point. In other words: he can show the mutiny (this is a good illustration of Iago's plan) or he can keep the mutiny from the public, that is to say not let the spectators in on the plan Shakespeare intended for Iago. In the first instance the whole figure of Iago, the horrible crime of Cassio, Othello's great love for Desdemona for the sake of which he flouts military discipline, all is increased in scale.

In the second instance, the whole shrinks to the dimensions of a small street brawl among drunks, instigated by a little, rascally intriguer, Iago—and Desdemona would scarcely show any power over Othello. It is this very reduction in scale which I have always found unbearable in all other productions that I have known of *Othello*.

It was only once, in the Hunting Club production, that I was able to produce it in the way I dreamed of. This was one of the most powerful moments in the play (it won the approval of Ernesto Rossi). You cannot conceive of how this small matter enhances the scale of everything that follows. If I were there with you it would be the easiest thing to prove the truth of my words, I feel this so strongly and I am so convinced of what I say. But at a distance I can only hold my tongue, and leave it to you to do what you can in accordance with your feelings. But I warn you that this is very harmful for the play. It will have an entirely different scale.

There is one bad thing—one has to include a crowd scene in a play one would like to keep intimate in tone. This is a great detraction, I agree. For my part I should do everything to minimize it. I should cut the crowd scene down to the size of the width of the gates, with the rest of it played down stage by some ten participants. Usually, however, I believe that one should not cut Shakespeare down but always expand him. . . .

(24 February 1930)

PART FOUR

"There is only one method—
that of organic, creative nature. . . ."

There is really no question of my method or your method. There is only one method, which is that of organic, creative nature... and I am willing to state in writing that if any student entering our theatre has anything to contribute towards a means of reaching the laws of that nature, I should be only too happy to learn from him.

(April 1936)

My system is for all nations. All peoples possess the same human nature: It manifests itself in varying ways, but my system is no deterrent to that.

—from one of Stanislavski's notebooks (1936)

The Theatre in Which the
Playwright Is Paramount

...Let us suppose a theatre in which the most powerful personality is the playwright or his representative, that is to say a literary director. This becomes a *literary theatre* in which the principal place is occupied by a carefully chosen repertory and subtle interpretations of a playwright's works.

In such theatres the interesting elements are: the general concepts of and approach to a play, the treatment of ideas, style, images, characters, psychology, etc. These are often based on solid knowledge, interesting commentaries, and sometimes they show a genuine literary maturity.... In every pause, intonation, gesture of an actor, in every line of the scene designs, in every object put on the stage, an idea is concealed, or some generalization, allegory, knowledge, etc. The playwright's works are so successfully revealed by the literary director of the play, or even by the playwright himself, that the other participants in the performance have nothing left to do except have confidence in their literary director, submit to his creative initiative, follow him blindly and do all they can to convey truly, concisely and beautifully the intent for the production of these outsiders. As a result you enjoy a large and honourable success, get serious reviews, stir arguments among the pundits, are the subjects of essays, etc.

Yet has this theatre fulfilled its fundamental objective in art, has it created the life of a human spirit and clothed it in a beautiful physical form? No! This is not within the bounds of its capabilities, and for this reason: An actor must live the life of his character every minute and with his own human emotions. The true and natural spirit of his part is created only by the true spirit of the actor, and sometimes is conveyed by direct radiation of feelings between two souls. Only the actor meets the spectator face to face, only he can enter into communion with the spectator.

Not even a genius can be expected to contain within himself the human emotions of all people, all directors, all their imaginative concepts and principles, some of which often derive not from feelings but from dry reason. Some thoughts you can grasp with your mind, but not everyone is capable of throwing his feelings into them. You can remember and execute the purely external instructions of the director, the things which have to do with acting movements, the *mise-en-scène*, the external production of one or another of the director's conceptions. An actor can comprehend with his mind the playwright's idea or the director's, and convey it to the public by external technical means, yet not participate with his soul in another person's treatment of the play.

But when we are discussing how to transmit genuine human emotions, the very soul of the playwright's or the director's idea, then the only medium between them and the public cannot be an actor's mind and technique, but only his own living emotions. There the actor must absolutely feel the emotions and sensations, or emotions and sensations analogous to those felt by the playwright or director. If the actor is capable of repeating these feelings through his emotion memory and if he keeps re-creating them, then he will be fulfilling the task set him by the director. But very often the soul of an actor is not amenable to being put into emotional, intellectual, scientific, theoretical and other patterns of accomplishment set by the director. The more subtle, complex, even talented a cultivated director's imaginative inventions may be, the harder will be the task of the actor. He needs an immense talent, a perfect technique, to be able even to some degree to catch up with divagations of the director's feelings, or the tangents of his imagination.

A director should bear firmly in mind that his objectives should not outdistance the creative faculties of his actors. Yet in the great majority of cases the directors do not reckon with the creative powers and potentialities of an actor, with his store of emotion memories, with the extent and creative power of his imagination. Most directors are far removed from the creative psychology of the actors, they are motivated exclusively by their own creative and often talented impulses.

That is why the major part of the innumerable tasks set by a director reach only an actor's mind and not his feelings. At best the actor will reduce the director's plan to its simplest proportions, or he may limit himself to making a beautiful literary recital of the play, or a rather pictorial rendering of its literary beauty—in other words he will limit himself to the representational form of acting. In the worst case, the blank spaces in his part, the parts which lack all feeling, will become infested with cliché; rubber-stamp, conventional clichés will be in the saddle and ride him.

This subservient attitude on the part of the actor forces him to renounce all expression of his creative individuality, it means for him complete subjection to the authority of his literary-minded director.

No artist of talent will be reconciled to this role of a simple reporter or go-between for the director and the spectator.

Therefore this playwright's theatre, predicated as it is on the despotism of the director-playwright, is doomed to be limited by the talent of this director-despot and be deprived of the talents of actors. In other words, in such theatres the dramatic art of the actor is completely nonexistent, and it is replaced by good or bad craft-acting. It will be only accidental when there is a coincidence between the creative emotions of the actor and the director which then results in moments of genuine creative artistry on the part of the actor.

The scientific dryness and lack of dramatic art in such theatres is compensated for by extreme intellectuality. There's a lot of intellect and little inspiration in them. Such literary theatres have their uses. They have culture, they spread knowledge, they develop literary taste, they make people think, they speak of higher things but, unfortunately, they are incapable of conveying the most important, most valuable things in our art, the things that can be communicated only by the means of the creative emotions of the individual actor, his successful contact with the public.

(Undated—revised in 1920's)

The Theatre in Which the
Scene Designer Is Paramount

There can be many combinations. Let us suppose for example, that the director is the strong figure in the theatre. Then the production plan moves into first place. The main emphasis is put on theatrical effect, plot, action. There will be much inventiveness, many stunts, plottings of various kinds and groupings—the effects will be the important part of the performance. The role of the actor will be relegated to that of an accessory subject to the uses of the director.

But there can be another combination. Let us suppose in this case that the scene designer is paramount. It is only natural that his talent will put the painting of the sets to the fore. The underlying thought and essence of the play will be sensed more vividly in colours, in the sets, in the painting-like compositions of group scenes. The stage will be converted into one great canvas and the theatre into an exhibition of the product of a painter. In this visual holiday the actor is scarcely more than a clothes horse for the artistic costumes of the painter and a rather poor illustrator of poses designed by the painter without regard for the human body, because he stylizes man according to the whim of his own fantasy, in lines that cannot be conveyed in action.

In theatres where scene designers are paramount the productions are converted into exhibitions of decorative canvases and picturesque costumes. Colours and lines create a feast for the eye and impose their supremacy on all aspects of the creative collective undertaking, they all come to serve the artist designer. This produces quite extraordinary inter-relationships, combinations, and approaches to the work of the playwright: it affects even the choice of plays and entire repertory of the theatre. Everything is done according to the whims of a capricious painter who has no regard for the principles of our art, nor even the very nature of the theatre and the creative evolution of the actor; all he is intent on are his own desires. In recent years more and more theatres have been founded on the tyranny of the scene designer, the despotism of a given painter. This is easily explained. Formerly the painter turned away from the theatre: now he is by right a working participant in our collective undertaking. There have been genuinely artistic productions, startling indeed in their external beauty and variety. The canvas background of a set is like a great sheet of paper which absorbs and reflects everything from vivid, high-relief, realistic truthfulness with its harsh, sharp lines, to the stylized conventions which have an unreal or impressionistic vividness, vague outlines, which have nothing to do with material considerations, and no flexible relation to the definite lines of the actual body of an actor. The work of a scene designer in such a theatre is self-sufficient, it excites the public and completely distorts the very approach to the play, the creative point of departure for its production and its relationship to the spectators. The whole centre of gravity is altered. The public, the director of the play, and the actors themselves fall prey to the enchantment and talent of the scene designer, and in their blindness they accept the foolish impositions which the painter is guilty of in relation to the playwright and his work, the actor and his art, indeed to the whole theatre itself.

Indeed the very repertory and choice of plays for production in such theatres depends on the scene designer who is working for them. They choose a painter of any school. In order to arouse his interest they offer him this or that production. But the painter is not so much interested in the content of the play as in the scope of decorative material it offers him. He makes his choice naturally, not on content but on epoch or style. For him the play offers a convenient opportunity to paint whatever interests and excites him most. If the painter has been in the Far East he may want an Oriental play, or if he has come from the country, or is interested in collections of objects and paintings from the past century, he will choose a play laid in the country about the third, fourth or fifth decade of the last century.... He is himself the all-important factor, he has the craving to stylize, individualize, let us say, his Egyptian impressions in the recent style of the decadent painters of the twenties.

If no special play can be found for a contemporary painter of extreme tastes, of a cubist or futurist slant, he will not hesitate arbitrarily and without rhyme or reason to convert Ostrovski, Shakespeare, Molière, Goldoni into cubists and futurists.

(Undated fragment)

An Argument with a Scene Designer

There was a time when scene designers were not known in the theatre, there was only a scene painter who worked on a yearly salary, and provided all that was needed in the way of scenery. From the artistic point of view that was a bad time. Finally, and to the joy of all, the artist painter came back to the theatre. In the beginning he was a modest inhabitant of the theatre, he kept quiet, as one would in another person's home, and was not in evidence, but gradually he began to lay hold of more and more power until in some theatres he came to play the chief role in undertaking a production, almost single-handed in its creation, and he edged the actor out of his legitimate part in the theatre. I myself had particular occasion to feel this when a famous artist, who was putting on a play in our theatre, mailed me a sketch of my make-up, together with categoric and strict remarks about how I was to put my make-up on. When I looked at the sketch I saw an entirely unknown person, quite the opposite of what the author intended, or that, under his influence, my imagination had prompted me to create. It turned out that the scene designer had not even read the text of the play we were producing, he had no conception of the complicated spiritual and analytical work that is done on a play and part, and that helps the actor to round out the creative process of merging himself body and soul with the nature of his part. The inconsiderate sketch prepared by the scene designer for me seemed miserable and his artistry really insulting.

It was a good thing that at least I was in an exceptional position, I thought, and could argue with this painter and stand up for my views. To be sure this was not easy to do even for me.

Yet it was possible. But imagine the position of an actor or a director "who dares not have his opinions" vis à vis the authority of the scene designer. In such a case one must feel both hurt and alarmed for the sake of one's art and the violence done to one's soul as an artist.

An actor may have created, become enamoured of, may have nurtured in his own heart a well-thought-out inner image which stirs his emotions, into which he throws himself body and soul. Then suddenly he receives a packet from Yalta or the Caucasus, from the same designer who is off there somewhere enjoying the charms of nature. The actor takes out of the package the portrait of a person entirely a stranger to him, and he is expected to conform his own image, the image he has created for his part with this stranger's physiognomy.

"I beg your pardon," the actor says shyly, "but I do not have the honour of this strange and uninviting gentleman's acquaintance."

"You have no business to argue, this is your make-up design!" says the voice from on high.

There is nothing left for the poor actor to do except to cut off the head with his own hands from his own image, and to fasten in its place this new head of an unknown and much disliked character. Will he be able to convey his own warm feelings through this inanimate mask? What happens in a case of such incompatibility?

Meanwhile the scene designer down in the Caucasus argues thus:

"This character, for whom I was ordered to design a make-up, is obviously a stupid man. Therefore I should give him a low forehead." Whereupon he designs one. "Moreover" he continues, "he is an aristocrat, so he has a refined nose and thin lips." His drawing now includes these items. "He is a dandy. Therefore he wears a small beard like the ones on a fashion plate man. Obviously he is wicked. So he has thin lips, is of dark complexion, has low eyebrows" etc. etc.

Now it could be that the actor had built his part on the idea of unexpected contrasts. He is wicked and a bright blond. He is an aristocrat but has a bulbous nose. He is stupid but has a high forehead with sparse hair.

When the actor meets the painter he cannot refrain from saying to him:

"It is not up to you to dictate to us. It is rather our feelings as actors, my own feelings as the person who has to play this particular character, who should dictate to you what is needed for the production. Your job is to acquire an insight into our conception, to understand its essentials, and let this suggest designs to you which are difficult for actors to explain in words. Neither you nor we, the actors, are independent agents in this enterprise. We are dependent on the playwright, and are in voluntary collaboration with him; you are dependent on the author and the actors, and you should voluntarily ally yourself with both."

Great heavens! What would be the reaction of the scene designer who considered himself the sole creator of the whole production? An actor telling me off. *Me*?! No indeed! I do not choose to be bothered with any such considerations. I go right ahead. What do I care whether or not an actor likes my design. It's enough to expect of me that I should waste my time in the theatre when I might be painting pictures.

"That means," I would retort, "that you are not one of us. You are a roomer who wants to run the boarding house. You do not need the theatre, the playwright, not Shakespeare, nor Gogol, not Salvini nor Ermolova. All you need is the frame of the theatre in which to exhibit your canvasses, your costumes. You need our faces on which to paint your designs instead of on canvas. And the whole—the theatre with us in it—you need only as a place for your own glorification. The theatre offers the easiest opportunity for that since thousands gather daily, whereas visitors in picture galleries are counted in tens. You would do better first of all to fall in love with the works of great poets, the great talents among artists, the particular art of the actor, with the very essence of which you perhaps are not familiar. And remember—no actors means no theatre, nor you in it. Come to us and work with us along with the directors of plays, with actors as they analyze plays, and come to know the life it enfolds. Help us in our joint creation, and when you, as a director or scene designer come to an understanding of the possibilities inherent in the available materials—acting and stage—then you can go to your own studio and give scope to your own inspiration. Then what you create will not be alien to us, for we shall have made common cause in our struggles and sufferings. But until such time as you fully realize what I am saying, and on what my feelings of indignation are based as an actor, you will be a stranger in our midst, an unwanted member of our family, a transient roomer in our home. Yet we are forever thirsting for a close bond with a real artist who will come to love us, who will understand the high mission of the theatre and of the art of the stage."

(Undated)

The Art of the Actor and the
Art of the Director

The art of the theatre has in all times been a joint enterprise, and this came about whenever the talent of the poet-playwrights worked in unison with the talents of the actors. At the base of each production there has always been some dramatic concept or other which unified the creativeness of the actor and lent to the action on the stage a general artistic significance. That is why the actor's creative process starts when he becomes immersed in the play. The actor should first of all, either independently or with the aid of the director, discover the fundamental motive of the play to be produced, the characteristic, creative idea of the given author, the *kernel* out of which his play naturally grew. The contents of a drama always bear the character of action unfolding before the public. In it the dramatis personae, according to their parts, participate in one way or another and develop in a given direction while striving always to move toward the final goal set by the playwright. This trying out, this uncovering of the kernel of the drama, and following the basic line of action through all the episodes—what we call the *through line of action* —all this represents the first phase of work for the actor and director. Let me say here that, in contrast to the attitude of certain other theatre people, I take the position that in the production of any significant and artistic play the director and actors must try to achieve an exact and profound understanding of the spirit and thought of the playwright and not replace them by their own inventions. The interpretation of a drama, and the character of its presentation in physical form on the stage is always, and inevitably, to some degree subjective, coloured by both the personal and national traits of the director and of the actors. It is only when profound attention has been paid to the artistic individuality of the playwright, to his ideas and moods which represent the life-giving kernel of his drama, that the theatre can plumb all the artistic depths and transmit its particular poetic essence, its integrity and harmony of proportion. Having arrived at this real kernel, which determines the through line of action of the play, all the participants in the future production will be drawn together by it in their creative work: each one to the extent of his capacities, will try to realize in terms of acting that same artistic goal which the playwright set himself in his medium of the art of literature.

Thus the actor's work begins with the search for the artistic kernel of a play. This he must transplant to his own soul and from that moment shall begin his creative process—the process which is akin to all organic growth in all aspects of nature. Set in the soul of an actor this kernel must begin to work, sprout, put down roots, put out shoots and, being nourished by the moisture of the earth into which it has been transplanted, grow into a flowering plant. This creative process can, in exceptional cases, take place very rapidly but usually if it is to be a genuine, living process and result in the creation of a living, vivid, truly artistic image—and not a hack imitation of one—much more time is necessary than is usually allowed even in the best European theatres. That is why in our theatre we do not put on a production after some eight or ten rehearsals, which is what the well-known German director and theorist K. Hagemann says is done there, but only after dozens of rehearsals which sometimes continue over a period of several months. Even under such circumstances an actor does not enjoy the same freedom as a writer does; an actor is circumscribed by the circumstances of his whole company, he cannot set aside his work until such time as his own physical and inner state is favourable for his creativeness. Meantime his artistic nature is both demanding and capricious; in a moment of inner exaltation he may receive impulses from his artistic intuition, which, when that creative state is not available, he cannot possibly recover by means of his conscious will. In this respect no external technique is of any avail, not control over his body, his mind or his voice. No external technique can replace the creative state in which intuition and imagination are released, and that state is not available on command.

Yet is it really not available? Are there no means which can arbitrarily, consciously, induce a creative state, which is available to geniuses because of their very nature and without their having to make any effort? If one cannot achieve this power by a single means, can one perhaps gain control step by step, by working out a series of exercises calculated to develop the elements out of which a creative state is compounded, and which are yet within the control of conscious will. This does not mean of course, that ordinary actors will, because of this, turn into geniuses, yet perhaps it may help them to approximate the qualities which distinguish geniuses. These are the questions which I set myself some twenty years ago in mulling over the inner obstacles which hamper our creativeness and often cause us actors as a result to have to resort to the use of crude rubber-stamp acting. This precipated my search for some method of *inner technique,* ways leading from the conscious to the subconscious, that realm where nine tenths of any genuine creative process takes place. By observing myself and other actors with whom I was rehearsing, and especially studying the great dramatic artists in Russia and abroad I was able to make certain generalizations which I then put into practice.

The first thing was that in any creative state an actor must have a fully free body, he must be entirely *free of muscular tensions* which unconsciously take hold of us when we are on the stage, and that also in ordinary life shackle us and interfere with our being subject to the dictates of our psychical activity. Thus muscular tension, which reaches its culmination when an actor is endeavouring to carry out some particularly difficult objective on the stage, absorbs an enormous amount of inner energy and diverts it away from the higher centres. Therefore if an actor can develop in himself the habit of freeing his body from superfluous tensions he removes one of the most substantial blocks to creative activity. This also means that he opens up the possibility of using the muscular energy of his various members only as needed and in precise proportion to what he is called on to do.

My second observation was that another factor which materially blocked the flow of an actor's creative powers, was his preoccupation with the auditorium, the public, the presence of which seems to constrict his inner freedom and keep him from devoting his entire attention to his objectives. Yet in watching the acting of great artists one cannot fail to note that their creative inspiration is always bound up with their concentration of attention on the action of the play itself, and also it is at this very time, when the actor's attention is not turned towards the public, that he acquires a special hold on them, a power over them, forcing them to participate actively in his artistic life. This does not mean of course, that an actor can entirely cease from sensing the presence of the public—the point is that the public should not oppress him or deprive him of the free quality of his creativeness. It is this last which the actor can achieve when he learns how to direct his attention. The actor who has the trained habit can limit his attention within a *circle of attention,* he can concentrate on whatever enters into that circle, and with only half an ear can listen to what transpires outside of it. In case of necessity he can even narrow the circle to produce a state we may call *public solitude.* But this circle of attention is usually flexible, it can be enlarged or shrunk by the actor in accordance with whatever must be included for the purposes of the stage action. Inside the limits of this circle there is an immediate and *central object of attention* of the actor as one of the dramatis personae—something on which his desire is for the moment centred, or another character in the play with whom, at this point of the play action, he is in close communion. Artistically the actor can only get the fullest value out of this *communion with an object* on the stage if he has trained himself in prolonged exercises so that he is capable of wholly receiving and wholly giving himself up to this communion, and also of absorbing it with a maximum of intensity. It is only then that action on the stage reaches its proper expressiveness; between the characters in the play a living bond is formed, such as is necessary in order to convey the drama to the fullest extent while always observing the right rhythm and tempo for the over-all performance.

Yet no matter what an actor's circle of attention may be—that is, whether it is lessened at times to put him into a state of *public solitude* or enlarged to contain all the characters on the stage— *creativeness on the stage, whether during the preparation of a part or during its repeated performance, demands complete concentration of all his physical and inner nature, the participation of all his physical and inner faculties.* This concentration includes his sight and hearing, all of his external senses, it stimulates not only the periphery but also the depths of his being, it challenges his memory, imagination, emotions, reason, will. The actor's entire spiritual and physical nature should be involved in what is happening to the character he has imagined. In moments of "inspiration," the spontaneous exaltation of all of his faculties, this is what happens to an actor. Contrarily, if he lacks this inspiration, an actor easily falls into the false paths beaten by centuries of theatrical traditions, he begins to "represent" an image seen somewhere, or perhaps only glimpsed in himself. He imitates the external manifestations of his feelings, or he attempts to "squeeze out" some emotions for his part, tries to "impress" himself with them. But when he thus violates his psychic organism with its immutable natural laws, he can never achieve any desired artistic results. He can only give a crude counterfeit presentment of an emotion, for emotions do not appear on demand. There are no efforts which the conscious will can make to arouse them directly, and nothing can be more sterile from the point of view of creativeness than to try to do this, to dig around in one's own soul. That is why one of the fundamental propositions for the actor who wishes to be a fine artist on the stage should be expressed as follows: *one cannot play or represent feelings, and one cannot call forth feelings point blank.*

Nevertheless, observation of the nature of gifted people does disclose to us a way to control the emotions needed in a part. This way lies through the action of the imagination, which to a far greater degree is subject to the effect of conscious will. We cannot directly act on our emotions, but we can prod our creative fantasy in a necessary path, and fantasy, as scientific psychologists have discovered, stirs up our *affective memory,* calling up from its secret depths, beyond the reach of consciousness, elements of already experienced emotions, and re-groups them to correspond with the images which arise in us. These images of our fantasy, which flare up without the slightest effort on our part, find a response in our affective (emotion) memory and the echo of appropriate feelings. That is why a creative fantasy is a fundamental, absolutely necessary gift for an actor. Without a well developed flexible fantasy no creativeness is possible—neither instinctive nor intuitive nor any sustained by an inner technique. In moments of exaltation it is stirred by a world of images dormant in the soul of an artist and often submerged deep in the realm of his subconscious.

Many and varied opinions have been expressed in public print to the effect that my artistic training of an actor, which uses the means of imagination to reach the affective (emotion) memory, which is to say an actor's own personal emotional experience, tends, for that very reason to limit the sphere of his creativeness to the extent of his own personal experience, and hence does not enable him to play parts which are not in harmony with his particular inner constitution. Such an opinion is based on the purest misunderstanding, for the same elements of reality out of which our fantasy shapes its unheard-of creations is also drawn from our own limited experience, whereas the richness and variety of these creations are achieved by the *combination* of elements drawn from experience. The musical scale has only seven notes, the sun's spectrum only seven primary colours, yet the combinations of those notes in music and those colours in paintings are not to be numbered. The same must be said of our fundamental emotions which are preserved in our affective (emotion) memory, just as things seen by us in the external world are preserved in our intellectual memory: the number of these fundamental emotions in our own inner experience is limited, but the shadings and combinations are as numerous as the combinations created out of our external experience by the activity of our imagination.

It is nevertheless a doubtless fact that an actor's inner experience, the circle of his impressions of life and sensations should be constantly enlarged, for it is only under such conditions that he can enlarge his sphere of creative accomplishment. On the other hand he must consciously develop his fantasy, trying it out on ever fresh tasks to perform.

Yet if an actor is to be emotionally involved and pushed into action on the stage by the imaginary world he builds on the basis of what the playwright has created, it is necessary that he believe in it as thoroughly as he does in the real world which surrounds him. This does not mean that while he is on the stage the actor must be subject to some kind of hallucination, that he must lose, while he is acting, the consciousness of surrounding reality, accept the canvas sets as real trees, etc. On the contrary a part of his consciousness must remain free from the trammels of the play in order that it exercise some supervision over whatever he is feeling and doing as he plays out the part of his character. He does not forget that his surroundings are stage sets and props, and nothing more than that, etc. but this has no significance for him.

It is as though he says to himself: "I know that everything by which I am surrounded on the stage is only a crude representation of reality, that it is all make-believe. But if it were real this is how I would relate myself to this manifestation, this is how I would act. . . ." And from the instant that his soul is aware of the magic phrase "if it were," the actual world around him ceases to interest him, he is carried off to another plane, to a life created by his imagination.

However, in giving himself up to it he may involuntarily alter its factualness both in his invented framework for that life and in the feelings related to it. His imaginary structure may prove illogical, untrue and then he will lose his faith in it. The feelings aroused by this image, his inner reactions to imagined circumstances may appear "contrived" and do not correspond to the nature of a given emotion. Finally in his expression of the inner life of his character, who is after all a complex human being, who has never been in sufficiently perfect control of his entire human apparatus, he may give a false intonation, may not observe a sense of artistic measure in his gesticulation, or he may be tempted to gain some cheap effect, he may become mannered or stilted. In order to ward off all these dangers which threaten the road of his stage creativeness an actor must without let-up work on the development of his *sense of truth,* which supervises all of his inner and physical activity both when he is creating and also when he is performing his part. It is only when his sense of truth is thoroughly developed that he will reach the point when *every pose, every gesture will have an inner justification,* which is to say they express the state of the person he is portraying and do not merely serve the purposes of external beauty, as all sorts of conventional gestures and poses do.

The sum total of the above-mentioned methods and habits constitute the inner technique of an actor. Parallel with its development should go the development of an external technique— the perfecting of a physical apparatus which serves to incarnate the stage image created by the actor for his part, and also express in precise and vivid ways the inner life of his character. With this purpose in mind the actor should train himself not only to physical flexibility and plasticity of movement, not only to smoothness and rhythm of motion, but also to a particular *consciousness of sovereign power over all his groups of muscles and the ability to feel the energy coursing through them,* which, coming as it does from his highest centres of creativeness, determines in a definite way his facial expressions, his gestures and, as it streams out from him, gathers in his partner acting opposite him on the stage, and also the public in the auditorium. It is incumbent on an actor to develop this keen awareness of and discrimination in his inner sensitiveness also in regard to his voice and speech. Our ordinary speech—both on and off the stage—tends to be prosaic, monotonous, our words sound choppy, they do not carry a vocal melody, an unbroken melody like that of a violin, which under the fingers of a master grows richer, deeper, lighter, more transparent, easily passing from high notes to low notes and back again, changing from *pianissimo* to *forte.* In trying to get away from the boring monotony of their reading actors ornament their speech, especially if they are reciting poetry. They resort to artificial vocal floweriness, cadences, abrupt lowering and raising of the voice, so characteristic of conventional high-flown elocution, which does nothing whatsoever to convey the emotions germane to the role, and consequently leaves with more perceptive listeners a sense of falseness. There does exist however, another *natural, musical, resonant form of speech* which we note in great actors in moments of genuine artistic inspiration, and which is deeply consonant with the inner music of the roles they are playing. An actor must acquire this musical speech for himself by exercising his voice under the control of his sense of truth almost to the same degree as a singer does. Along with this he must work on his diction. An actor can have a powerful, flexible, expressive voice and nevertheless distort his speech either by indistinct diction or a negligent attitude towards the scarcely perceptible pauses and accents by which one conveys the exact meaning of a phrase, and also determines its emotional colouring. In a perfect piece of playwriting every word, every letter, every punctuation sign serves to transmit its own inner essence; an actor who is interpreting a drama in the terms of his own understanding of it, will attach to each phrase his individual shadings conveyed not only by the expressiveness of his body, but also by an artistically trained speech. Nor may we forget that each sound which forms a word, each vowel as well as each consonant is, as it were, a separate note which takes its place in the tonal chord of a word, it expresses this or that small part of the soul that filters through the word. That is why any work on the perfecting of the phonetic side of speech cannot be limited to mere mechanical exercises of the organs of speech; it must also be aimed at teaching the actor to *feel each distinct sound of a word as a means to artistic expressiveness.* In this respect however, as also in respect to any musical quality of voice, freedom, plasticity and rhythm of movement, as well as in general all external techniques of theatre art, not to mention inner techniques, the actor of our times is still on a very low level of artistic culture. He lags far behind the masters in the field of music, poetry, painting and he has before him a long road of development.

Obviously, under these circumstances, the production of any play that could meet with high standards of art, cannot be completed with the rapidity which economic factors impose on the vast majority of theatres. The creative process through which every actor must go, beginning with his first conception of his part and ending with his artistic embodiment of it, is in itself very complicated, and is further delayed by the inadequacies of his inner and external techniques. Moreover the pace is definitely slowed up by the necessity of adjustments between the actors, the harmonizing of individualities and the welding of them into one artistic whole.

The responsibility for creating this ensemble, for its artistic integrity, the expressiveness of the over-all performance lies with the director. In the period when the director was a despot—and this began with the Meiningen Theatre and has lasted up to now, even in some of our more advanced theatres—he worked out the whole plan of the production, he indicated the general outlines of the parts, taking into consideration of course the participating actors, and he showed them all the "business." Until recent years I myself adhered to this way of producing plays. But now I have arrived at the conviction that the creative work of the director must proceed in unison with that of the actors and not outdistance it nor hold it back. He must facilitate the creativeness of the actors, supervise and integrate it, taking care that it evolves naturally and only from the true artistic kernel of the play. This applies also to the external shaping of a performance. That should be, in my opinion, the objective of a director nowadays.

This joint work of the director and the actors, this search for the essential kernel of the play, begins with analysis and proceeds along the line of *through-going action*. Later comes the determination of the through line in each role—that fundamental impetus of each part which as it derives naturally from its character, fixes its place in the general action of the play. If the actor does not at once sense this main direction of his part he must be helped in this by the director, who will break down the role into smaller units which correspond to the unfolding phases in the life of the given character to be portrayed; he will also divide it into *separate objectives* which the actor is to attain in working toward his ultimate goal. In case of necessity these separate units, as well as objectives, can be subjected to still further psychological analysis, and broken down into more detailed bits to correspond with the desired actions of the character, and out of which his life on the stage is composed. But what the actor must seek is not emotions or moods which inform and embellish each of these fragments, but the volitional *mainspring* of those emotions and moods. In other words, as the actor thinks about each small unit of his part he should ask himself what he desires, what he is attempting to achieve in the person of the character he is playing, and what concrete small objective he is setting himself at a given moment. His answer to that question should not be expressed in the form of a noun, it must be formulated as a verb: "I wish to conquer the heart of this woman," "I wish to penetrate into her home," "I wish to *get rid of* the servants guarding her," etc. If he formulates a desired objective this way, its object and setting will acquire a more vivid and distinct image for the actor, because his creative fantasy will be put to work. He will become involved, affected; the combination of feelings needed for his part will be lured out of the depths of his memory-feelings, which possess the quality of efficacy and spill over into dramatic action. Thus the actor finds that the individual bits of his role come to life, are enriched by the spontaneous interplay of complex, organic emotions. When they are gathered up and grow together, these separate units form the *score of a role*; the scores of separate roles, after constant work together during rehearsals, and after the necessary adjustments to each other have been made by the actors, finally merge into the *score of the whole performance*.

Yet even now the work of the actors and the director is not at an end. As he thinks more deeply about his part and gets farther into it, discovering ever more profound artistic motivations, the actor feels its whole score in richer tones. Meanwhile both the score of his part and of the production as a whole undergo further change as more work is done on them: just as in a perfect piece of poetry there are no superfluous words, only those necessary to the artistic content, *so in the score of a role there should not be a single superfluous feeling, only what is needed for the purpose of a through line of action*. The score of each role must be condensed, the form of its conveyance be made concrete; vivid, simple significant forms must be found for its physical embodiment. It is only when all these feelings naturally mature and come to life in every actor, when they are purged of all extraneous matter and crystallized, when all parts have been composed into a general tone, rhythm and tempo—it is only then that the production may be presented to the public.

As the performances are repeated, the stage score of the play, as well as that of each part, no longer changes in general form. Yet this does not mean that from the moment the production has been shown to the public one can consider that the creative process of the actors is finished, that all they have to do is to repeat mechanically their opening performance. On the contrary, each successive performance requires that they be in a creative state, all their inner faculties must participate in their acting, because it is only under these conditions that they will be able to adjust the scores of their parts to the capricious mutations which are constantly taking place in them every hour of the day and night, as they do in every being with a nervous system, and by the contagion of their emotions spread to each other, they convey to the public things which are visible and ineffable, the spiritual content of a drama. Therein lies the essence of art in the theatre.

As for the outer form of a production—the stage sets, the props, etc.—all that is of value only to the extent that it promotes the expressiveness of dramatic action, the art of the actor; and it should under no circumstances whatsoever draw the public because of any independent artistic quality, something which great artists among our scene designers have wished to do right up to the present time. Stage sets, as well as incidental music are only auxiliary, supporting factors in theatre art, and it is the duty of the director to draw from them only what is necessary to illuminate the drama being unfolded before the public, and to see that they remain subservient to what the actors are called upon to do.

—Written for the *Encyclopedia Britannica* (Late 1920's)

PART FIVE

"Memories of the Past . . .
Dreams of the future"

He took from life all that it can give to a man, yet all these impressions, passions, satisfactions, all that others use for their own lives, were transformed by him into materials for creativeness. . . .
—written for the Goethe Centennial (1932)

The life of an artist is not passed on the plane of everyday life but in his beautiful memories of the past and his dreams of the future. . . .
—from a letter to Max Reinhardt (1928)

A Better Mousetrap

. . . You ask me to recall and write you when and in what circumstances I gave photographs of myself to Anton Pavlovich. I cannot remember this but I shall try to bring back something of the surrounding considerations.

I blushed when I read over the inscriptions listed in your note. They were such dry, formal phrases. Now that the memory of dear Anton Pavlovich has become a cult for all of us the cold tone of my dedications seems inexcusable to me. How is this to be explained?

One of the photographs was dated January 17, 1904, which was his birthday and also the date of the opening of *The Cherry Orchard*. This was an unforgettable and terrifying day; our opening, a wonderful new play, a new role, a new production of our theatre, a birthday anniversary and finally—[our concern over] Anton Pavlovich's health! Everything frightened us.

But beyond all our worries I was also concerned with a present for Chekhov's birthday. What would give pleasure to Anton Pavlovich? A silver pen for him as a writer, or an antique inkwell? What would he do to me if I offered him either of those? A piece of old, gold embroidered material? What would he do with that? But I could think of nothing better so I sent the photographs to him with a wreath.

"I haven't any study any more! It's a museum now," complained Chekhov.

"Well, what should I have given you?" I enquired.

"A mousetrap! We do have mice! Now Korovin sent me a fishhook. Listen, that's a marvelous present!"

Those are the circumstances in which I signed my photographs. Perhaps this will serve as my excuse. . . .

> To Maria Pavlovna Chekhova (sister of Anton Chekhov)
> (3 January 1935)

A Theatre for All

... In art there is the passing fashion and there is what is lasting. What is lasting never dies, whereas the fashion of the moment fades away leaving but little trace. What we see around us is temporary, ephemeral. It is not without its use because from it a small crystal is formed, probably a very small one, which will fuse its small accomplishments with what is eternal in art and add a push ahead. All the rest will be irretrievably lost.

All that we have been living through will undoubtedly create a new literature which will mirror the new life of the people. New actors will reproduce this new life in terms of the eternally unchanging laws, common to all of us in the field of creativeness. These laws have been studied with relation to the technique of acting ever since far distant times in the past, and this has been enriched by all that is contributed to art, all the latest searchings of the serious innovators in our profession.

Do not show this letter to anyone as my opinion is quite superficial and unfounded and might mislead people who like to be clever about art rather than use their own feelings. . . .

To N. V. Volkonskaya (12 October 1924)

... People come into the theatre for entertainment but, without their being aware of it, they leave it with awakened emotions and thoughts, enriched by the experience of having witnessed the beautiful life of a human spirit.

The impressions received in the theatre are irresistible because they are not produced by the art of the actor alone but by all the contributing arts taken together; it is the simultaneous effect of a great number of people working together to produce a performance.

The power of the theatre is in the fact that it is a joint enterprise, uniting in one harmonious whole the creative work of writers, poets, actors, directors, musicians, dancers, participants in crowd scenes, scene designers, lighting staffs, costumers, and all the other contributors to a theatre production. This is a great, massive and well-equipped force which acts together, moves together to make its impression on the mass of spectators, causing thousands of human hearts to beat as one. The highly charged atmosphere of the theatre draws out a contagious mass emotion. Besides, the spectators hypnotize each other and thus heighten the impact from the stage.

Thanks to all these qualities of our art it is more easily acceptable to people than any other single art. The reading of books requires that one be literate, to understand what is read aloud requires habit, musical subtleties are clear only to the specialists, a mute statue or painting may say a lot to the soul of an artist but what it says may not always be understood by an ordinary viewer. But theatre art is so vivid, so full of imagery, it so fully illustrates the plays offered, that its form is accessible to everyone, from the professor to the peasant, from the young to the aged. . . .

(1917)

. . . The idea of bringing actors from all nations together occurred to me too when I was on tour for two years with the Art Theatre in Europe and America. I saw with my own eyes that everywhere the theatre is passing through a severe crisis.

To begin with, it has been undermined by the cinema, then given the final blow by the war; it has been forced to cater to sharply lowered standards of taste due to the emergence at this time of a special class of speculators who abound in all the big cities and set the tone for all. It is to suit their tastes that the contemporary theatre is adapting its repertoire of plays and productions. For their sake there is a show of unheard-of luxury, an abundance of tawdry, spectacular inventions, naked women, and vulgar texts, emulating the cinema.

I have been struck by the fact that the persons who govern these countries, who presumably are concerned with the ethical, moral, and aesthetic development of the peoples under their aegis . . . have forgotten the high significance of the theatre. They have practically crossed off its educational and uplifting qualities as an influence on the masses, and have consigned it to merely the role of superficial entertainment, a means of distracting the people from politics.

In a conversation with one highly placed person, whose name I do not feel I can mention because our talk was a private one, he quite frankly stated: "I must warn you that I despise the theatre."

"Which one?" I asked. "The one that is depraved, low-minded? If so, I despise it even more than you do. Or is it the high-minded, noble theatre which should serve, under any government, as one of the best and principal means of bringing about reconciliation and mutual understanding between nations?" After that we went into a prolonged and fervent discussion of the theatre as one of the means of leading to the achievement of world peace, a goal which now, since the end of the war, is being talked about in all corners of the globe.

In almost all countries where I have had to act in a tongue foreign to my audiences, and before a public unknown to me, in plays totally unfamiliar to them and brought from a completely alien land far off to the East, I heard these words repeatedly: "One such performance says more to us than all the conferences, expeditions, congresses, lectures, scientific treatises, which endeavour to define the soul of another people so that we may become better acquainted with them."

This capacity of the theatre is easy to understand. If a writer, who is a national genius, expounds fully a theme to describe the most characteristic and profound traits of the soul of his people, if his work is presented by the most gifted actors of his land, working with its best directors, scene designers and the other master technicians of our cooperative art, it is bound to reveal the soul of his people, the details of their life, the things that affect their psychology. And if these interpreters appear in person in foreign countries and convey from heart to heart their own spiritual nature, then it is not astonishing that this art, this performance, is bound to transmit even more fully the invisible, the intangible human feelings which are beyond consciousness yet which are, above all, necessary to the knowledge and understanding of a foreign people and their land. This is something no scientific report, no lecture, no treatise, no conference, nor even the inert letters of a book or newspaper, can achieve.

They have their own field of operation in transmitting the printed word. But in the area available to the actor an invisible light is conveyed from soul to soul.

I told this unnamed person . . . that it is on such as he that the obligation rests for [the creation of] such a theatre, a theatre for humanity, a theatre for mutual understanding.

—from a letter to Firmin Gémier (April 1926)

. . . The time will come, and very soon, when a great play, a work of genius, will be written. It will, of course, be revolutionary. No great work can be anything else. But this will not be a revolutionary play in the sense that one will parade around with red flags. The revolution will come from something inside. We shall see on the stage the metamorphosis of the soul of the world, the inner struggle with a worn-out past, with a new, not yet understood or realized present. This will be a struggle for equality, freedom, a new life, and a spiritual culture, the extinction of war. . . .

This is the time when we need real actors who know how to express themselves, not just in words, vocal effects, but also with their eyes, inner urgencies, beams of feelings, great efforts of will. This play will call for entirely new settings, furnishings, not the kind I have favoured for so long and which have come to be known under the cliché of "Stanislavski's naturalism." Nor the kind considered new and in the current fashion. These future settings will be quite different, of the kind that will not obstruct the Actor (with a capital A). But where will this Actor be found? I assert that his place of origin is here, and only here, in our theatre family. But in saying this, I am not limiting this family merely to our country, I include the whole world.

For the time is coming, and soon, when only the *fine theatres* will be in existence. All the rest, the mediocre ones, will pass into the hands of the cinema. . . . Theatres will have to pull themselves together or they will be jettisoned. . . . Nevertheless the cinema will never be able to compete with a live, creative human being who not only speaks but also *radiates*. This capacity can never be put on films and the only actors who have this technique are those of our theatre.

The tradition of this art still lingers within the walls of our theatre. It is deeply implanted in the souls of our old members, of whom some unconsciously acquired our art. They know no other. But we are getting old, and therefore I should wish to see all the young members, those who are to replace us, make use of us before it is too late, while we can still talk and teach.

Put your minds more deeply on what the older actors say, ask more questions, try to understand what you learn from us. And take your places beside us in front of the footlights more often. The things I am talking about are not learned just in the class-room, in rehearsals, or in working at home. They are learned principally in front of the footlights, before a full auditorium, heart to heart, in the very moment of creativeness. . . .

—Remarks to the Moscow Art Theatre Company
(31 December 1929)

The View at Seventy

. . . Illness prevents my being with all of you who wished to honour me with a seventieth birthday celebration. I appreciate all the more the honour you wished to show me and the kind impulses that prompted you because I know how difficult it is to get up such a celebration. One reason I refused to have any official celebration was to prevent overtiring the already exhausted actors by having them make extra public appearances. In spite of this you chose to gather today. I am all the more touched and my feelings of gratitude are even deeper to all the initiators of the celebration, those who took part in it and their guests. My principal and deepest bow is to all of them. . . .

In such times as these, when human hearts and minds are stirred by historic events, it is a difficult thing to hold together a large group of people bound by a common idea. We artists and actors are lucky because we are held together by art, which in history-making times is even more necessary than ever to the inner life of the people. Yet there is no area, other than art, where there are such divergent opinions, views, trends, "methods," discoveries, disagreements, hostility and quarrelsome feelings. All these are divisive elements. Yet despite them all we are bound one to another. People may say that what unites my comrades in art, my pupils, and those who share my ideas . . . is the "Stanislavski System." What system?

By now, in every theatre that has sprung from the Moscow Art Theatre, this system has been transformed into something different, new, even contrasting. Yet in spite of this we are not strangers to one another, we are still bound by something and it leads us along the path of art.

What is this bond? This bond is in the system, not that of Stanislavski, but that of the greatest creative artist of all—Dame Nature. She and her fundamental laws are binding on all alike, on people of all trends and interpretations of true art. To the extent that we are in touch with these creative laws we are closely allied with one another. To the extent that we move away from nature into the realm of innumerable conventions we become strangers and cease to understand one another.

I write all this in order to put our bond into a clearer, more exact and definite form. I have devoted all my activity in the theatre not to the creating of some new art invented by me, but only to the most detailed, painstaking study of the creative nature of the person-artist in myself, in other actors, in my students, in amateurs, in musicians and singers. My work is not that of invention but of research. It has not been done in vain. This is proven by today's gathering of my friends, comrades in art, fellow-workers, and pupils all united in a common faith in that so-called system of the nature of man. Only nature is eternal, understood by all, a necessity to all who choose to approach art.

My second bow is to my friends, those who share my ideas in recognition of the idea that unites us all in art.

Throughout the world, theatres are in a state of crisis and even in our country all is not well in the field of art; yet thanks to the efforts of our government art is not dying, it is moving ahead. When we think of the future and of our dangerous rival the cinema, we can sense the dark outlook for all bad theatres in the world. They will have to give way to the great once silent, and now painfully strident, giant.

Nevertheless I see the future of the theatre as rosy. There will be fewer theatres but those that survive will be magnificent in their true art, and that true art will stem straight from the laws of creative nature. Those who study and follow those laws may rest assured for they will not be threatened by any danger, they can look forward to the dawn of renewal. Those who have abandoned nature had better return to her as quickly as they can.

Human nature is infinitely varied, therefore its laws will give rise to innumerable varieties and trends in art. So much the better. This should be very much welcomed. Because if all aspects of art were as alike as two drops of water, it would be a bore; and there is nothing worse in the world than art which is boring.

So let everyone create in his own way, according to his own desires and capabilities, let him do as he chooses, let him paint as many eyebrows and marks on his face as he likes—providing only that what he does is justified from within and in accordance with the eternal laws of nature which are binding on all.

My third bow is to those who share our ideas and who have played a great part in saving the moribund art of the actor by returning it to the realm of that forever young and never-fading artist—Dame Nature.

—To the members of the Moscow Art Theatre (January 1933)

. . . I do not know how to reply to your remarkable letter. I do not have the necessary words in my lexicon, and besides I rather fear my answer will prove pale in comparison to your message.

I should be very presumptuous if I attributed to my own merits all the flattering and even at times overwhelming things you write about me. Whatever accrues to my credit I must in all fairness share with Nemirovich-Danchenko and my friends the "elders" of the theatre who have worked with me for so long. And half of what might be my share should be attributed to your generosity—which is characteristic of you—and to your capacity, as a great artist, for enthusiasm. . . .

My life has been a fortunate one. It shaped itself. I was just a tool in its hands. Yet this good fortune lays on me the obligation to hand on to others, before I die, what life has given to me. Yet how difficult it is to share one's experience in such a complex process as the creative work of an actor. When one is in personal touch with students one can show, demonstrate, act out things which are difficult to formulate in written words. To act out— that is our sphere. But when one takes pen in hand all the words needed to define feelings run away and hide themselves. Since the time when we were together in Capri and you had the energy to plough through my initial notes, my attempts to wield a pen in an effort to set down something in the nature of a Grammar of Acting, I have harnessed my mind to the task of putting on paper, as concisely and clearly as I can, what a beginning actor should know. Such a book is needed if only to put an end to all the twisted interpretations put on my so-called "system" which, in the way it is presently being taught, can put young actors on quite the wrong path. . . . If only I could shed ten years off my age and get rid of this everlasting invalidism! Yet to be well I have to be in a warm climate, and if I go to a warm climate I cannot work, and if I cannot work, why live?

—from a letter to Maxim Gorki acknowledging
his seventieth birthday salute (10 February 1933)

Index

INDEX

INDEX